KNOW WHAT YOU BELIEVE (THE BASICS)

Grace Pathway 3.3

BILL GIOVANNETTI

ISBN E-book edition: 978-1-946654-19-9

ISBN Print edition: 978-1-946654-18-2

For additional resources, please visit maxgrace.com.

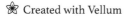 Created with Vellum

CONTENTS

THE BASICS // GOD'S TRUTH

All Scripture is given by inspiration of God, and is profitable for doctrine, for reproof, for correction, for instruction in righteousness, that the man of God may be complete, thoroughly equipped for every good work. (2 Timothy 3:16, 17)

I f you've ever had a sweater with a loose thread, you've probably noticed something. Some threads are no problem. You pull on them till they lock up, then you snip them off.

No big deal.

But other loose threads aren't so easy. If you pull on them, the whole sweater comes unravelled.

It's the same way with basic teachings in the Bible. Some of them won't cause huge issues if we don't get them right. But there are other teachings in the Bible that are so important, if we get them wrong, the whole message of Christ comes unravelled.

In this book, I want to introduce you to those most important teachings of the Bible. I want to help you know what you believe, and why you believe it.

To do that, let's nail down some terms.

DOCTRINE

The word *doctrine* simply means teaching. Doctrine especially refers to biblical teachings that have a technical term attached to them, like the doctrine of justification, or the doctrine of propitiation. We met both of those doctrines in *The Cross,* book 3.2 in the Grace Pathway Series.

I love doctrine! Doctrine is God's gift to us. It is a gift that makes truth clear, and organized, and consistent. Doctrine also lets us think deep thoughts about God, his world, and our lives. It is how we grow mature in our understanding, and in our whole lives. And it is how we organize the Bible's teaching, topic by topic.

The more you know doctrine, and doctrinal terms, the more you can read any part of your Bible with confidence and understanding.

CARDINAL DOCTRINES

Another helpful term is the term *cardinal*. No, not the bird, and no, not the religious leaders of Catholicism.

Cardinal means "of chief importance." Some doctrines are cardinal doctrines and some doctrines are not. The cardinal doctrines are the ones that unravel the whole sweater if you get them wrong.

In this book, I want to introduce you to the cardinal doctrines. Consider these the core of our faith.

They are the basics of everything we believe as Christians.

The cardinal doctrines are the heart of the heart of what we believe and of who we are.

Everything we believe and everything we teach has to come from Scripture. More than that, it has to come from the clear and abundant teaching of Scripture. You can't pick out obscure Bible verses and put together doctrines from them.

When God reveals his heart on a topic, he makes it super-clear. He weaves his most important truths throughout many places in Scripture. That way, we can't miss his message.

TRUTH FITS WITH TRUTH

One last thing before we get into the basics.

One of the most beautiful discoveries you will make as you grow along God's Grace Pathway is that God's truths all fit together. They mesh perfectly. They make sense together. And they help us see the beautiful intricacy and unity not only of God's Word, the Bible, but of God's omnipotent and gracious heart.

The basic doctrines we cover in this book are not random. They have bubbled to the top over centuries of Christian experience. You will find them stated by most churches and faith-based organizations in their official statements of faith.

There are many places where faithful, Bible-believing Christians will disagree. As we go along, I will point those out. It's important to be respectful and kind in our differences.

But there are some truths so important that to deny them is to be unfaithful to Christ. I will point out those truths, too.

At the end of it all, God does not give us a final exam on our doctrine before he lets us into heaven. We can be wrong on a whole lot of things, but if we have placed our faith in

Jesus as our Savior and only hope, then we are God's children forever.

Now, let's grow deep. It's time to dig into the basics of our faith.

LET THERE BE LOVE

There are reasonable, Bible believing Christians who can draw different conclusions on the different topics of the Bible. That's okay.

There's an old motto I heard back in seminary days.

In essentials, unity. In non-essentials, diversity. In all things, charity.

The purpose of doctrine is to clarify and sometimes to divide. But our division is never to be nasty or rude, and never tinged with superiority or condemnation.

Christians can agree to disagree without being disagreeable!

Let's model that "doctrine" to everyone we see.

———

JUST A QUICK WORD ABOUT PROCEDURE. To form the foundation of this book, I have chosen the official Statement of Faith of the seminary I was privileged to attend, Trinity Evangelical Divinity School (TEDS), in Deerfield IL.[1] There are countless excellent statements of faith, but I chose this one for several reasons. I wholeheartedly endorse it, it's the right length for these purposes, and it hits the ball of what is called *evangelical* theology right down the middle of the fairway.

I belong to this evangelical tribe, because I am utterly convinced it does the best job of interpreting, summarizing, and respecting what the Bible actually says. At the same time,

4

I am not suggesting that there are no saved or sincere Christians outside of evangelicalism. This, however, is my tribe, and its doctrines are most precious to me.

The TEDS statement contains ten paragraphs. These begin every chapter of this book but two. I have added two additional chapters—chapter 6 on Creation, and chapter 11 on Satan and Demons—which are not covered in the TEDS statement, but I felt were essential to introduce to students along the Grace Pathway.

FINAL NOTE. Shortly before this book went to press, the Evangelical Free Church of America, the presiding organization over TEDS, revised its doctrinal statement on the return of Christ. That revision is noted in chapter 12.

------

1. Trinity Evangelical Divinity School, "Statement of Faith," retrieved July 2019. https://divinity.tiu.edu/who-we-are/statement-of-faith/

THE BIBLE // GOD'S BOOK

> *We believe that God has spoken in the Scriptures, both Old and New Testaments, through the words of human authors. As the verbally inspired Word of God, the Bible is without error in the original writings, the complete revelation of His will for salvation, and the ultimate authority by which every realm of human knowledge and endeavor should be judged. Therefore, it is to be believed in all that it teaches, obeyed in all that it requires, and trusted in all that it promises.*

There is no book like the Bible. No other sacred literature, and no work of philosophy, in all the ages of humankind, can compare.

If you want a book of moral precepts to guide us into love and respect for one another, there is no book like the Bible.

If you want an origin story that dignifies the human race as created in the image of God, there is no book like the Bible.

If you want a revelation of a God who not only shows love, but is love, there is no book like the Bible.

If you want a book that satisfies our intellectual curiosity while simultaneously fulfilling our emotional needs, there is no book like the Bible.

The Bible is God's love-letter to the world. It is his message of truth and grace to us. Its power is peerless, its scope is limitless, and its truth is timeless.

From cover to cover, the Bible lays bear God's heart, calling us to infinity and beyond in relationship to him.

Search the sacred literature of all the world. Comb through the annals of history. Study the finest points of religion and philosophy. You will never find a compendium of meaning, truth, realism, and hope that can even begin to compare to the Bible. There is nothing like it.

Here are the top three cardinal doctrines the Bible teaches about itself.

***

INSPIRATION

The Bible was written by about forty human authors. At the same time, we believe it was written by God. How can both be true?

Both are true because of a super-important teaching called Inspiration. First, I'll give you a simple definition, then we'll talk about it.

 INSPIRATION: God personally oversaw the writing of Scripture, working through the personality and setting of each human author, so that what they wrote were the exact words God intended, perfectly transmitting his message.

The Bible truly is God's book. It is of both supernatural and human origin.

Inspiration does not mean that God put the authors of Scripture into a trance. It does not mean he dictated each word to them and they wrote it down like robots.

Instead, inspiration means God supernaturally influenced the writers, so that they perfectly conveyed his message in their own personality, style, and vocabulary.

> All Scripture is given by inspiration of God, and is profitable for doctrine, for reproof, for correction, for instruction in righteousness, (2 Timothy 3:16)

Inspiration is the cornerstone of what evangelical Christians believe.

Peter tells us that when the authors of Scripture wrote, their writings "never came by the will of man, but holy men of God spoke as they were moved by the Holy Spirit" (2 Peter 1:21).

Jesus respected all of Scripture as the Word of God, and we should too.

In a weird twist, Christians who take the Bible seriously, are often accused of actually worshipping the Bible.

No. Never.

We simply believe when we read the Bible we are reading the inspired message of God, that we might understand, believe, know, worship, and obey him.

VERBAL INSPIRATION

To go even deeper, we also believe that God inspired the very words of Scripture. Some people suggest that God inspired the ideas, but not the words. But I would ask, how could inspired ideas be conveyed in uninspired words?

God inspired even the fine points of the biblical text. One excellent example happens when the New Testament is equating the Old Testament word "seed" with Jesus Christ. In Galatians 3:16, Paul quotes from Genesis 22:18. In Genesis, God promises to bless Abraham's "seed."

In Galatians, Paul points out that "seed" is singular, not plural in Genesis. He is arguing his case from whether a noun is singular or plural in the Old Testament. Think about what that means. If God only inspired the ideas, but not the words, Paul could never make that case!

> The entrance of Your words gives light; It gives understanding to the simple. (Psalm 119:130)

We believe that every single word of the Bible is inspired by God. The word for this is *Verbal* inspiration, based the Latin word, *verbum,* which means word.

We believe the whole Bible is verbally inspired.

INERRANCY

Inspiration naturally leads to another important quality of God's Word.

If God is perfect, then his book is perfect too. We believe the Bible is without error. This is called Inerrancy.

> *INERRANCY: God's Word is perfect and without error in all that it teaches on every subject it addresses.*

Whatever God affirms is real and true.

Whatever God denies is unreal and false.

Wherever the Bible touches history, archaeology, theology, science, psychology, philosophy, sociology, or any other field, the Bible is perfectly true all the time.

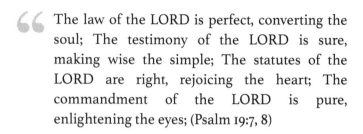

> The law of the LORD is perfect, converting the soul; The testimony of the LORD is sure, making wise the simple; The statutes of the LORD are right, rejoicing the heart; The commandment of the LORD is pure, enlightening the eyes; (Psalm 19:7, 8)

Some Bible scholars suggest the Bible may contain errors. They say that the Bible is perfect when it talks about God and salvation, but might make some mistakes when it talks about other things. They'll go on to argue that this is okay, because all we really care about is salvation and the religious teachings of Scripture.

There is a huge problem with this view.

All the teachings of the Bible fit together, like a complex Lego structure. You can't take out one piece without disrupting the whole thing. You can't separate one kind of biblical teaching from another. They all fit together and support each other to create a perfect and beautiful whole.

Besides that, Jesus himself said that "the Scripture cannot be broken" (John 10:35). Referring to little marks in the Hebrew alphabet, like the dot on an i and the cross on a t, Jesus also said, "For assuredly, I say to you, till heaven and earth pass away, one jot or one tittle will by no means pass from the law till all is fulfilled" (Matthew 5:18).

The bottom line is simple: you can trust your Bible. Every part of it. You don't have to pull out the errors like bones from a fish, because there are none.

AUTHORITY

If God has spoken decisively in his Word, and if that Word is final, complete, and verbally inspired, then it follows that God's Word is the ultimate and final authority in our lives.

Everything we believe has to pass the test of Scriptures. Don't believe something just because a pastor says it. Don't believe something just because a priest, Pope, pastor, or Ph.D. says it.

Don't believe something because it's popular, or because it's culturally correct.

Don't even believe something because your emotions want it to be true. Emotions can lie to you, but the Word of God stands true.

Test every doctrine against Scripture.

Scripture is the final authority. There is no higher court of appeal.

There is one viewpoint that says the Church is higher than the Scriptures, since the Church wrote the Scriptures. That is wrong, and let me show you why.

First, three-fifths of the Bible was already complete by the time Jesus launched his church. It's called the Old Testament, and there were no Popes or ecclesiastical authorities that were ever seen as having more authority than it.

There's an even more convincing story from the early days of the church.

When the early apostles visited a certain city, they taught the truth of Jesus. However, the people in that town refused to take their word for it. They insisted on evaluating the validity of their teaching by the Scriptures! These were the *apostles*, the highest early leaders in Christianity, and even *they* were subject to the Bible.

> Then the brethren immediately sent Paul and Silas away by night to Berea. When they arrived, they went into the synagogue of the Jews. These were more fair-minded than those in Thessalonica, in that they received the word with all readiness, and searched the Scriptures daily to find out whether these things were so. (Acts 17:10, 11)

They "searched the Scriptures" — the everyday people of the church did that, without possessing degrees or ordinations.

"To find out whether these things" — meaning the apostolic teaching— "were so" — the highest leaders of the church were subject to evaluation by the written Word of God as interpreted by the everyday people of God.

Why?

Because our verbally inspired and inerrant Bible is the final and supreme authority for our faith, our relationships, our opinions, and for everything in our lives. It has more authority than all our churches, our pastors, and our priests put together.

The Bible is all the truth we need for faith and life.

THERE'S an old song I used to sing as a little kid in church. It still speaks my love language. Find the tune online, and sing along. Here you go.

The Bible stands like a rock undaunted
'Mid the raging storms of time;
Its pages burn with the truth eternal,
And they glow with a light sublime.

The Bible stands tho' the hills may tumble,
It will firmly stand when the earth shall crumble;
I will plant my feet on its firm foundation,
For the Bible stands,

The Bible stands.
The Bible stands like a mountain tow'ring
Far above the works of man;
Its truth by none ever was refuted,
And destroy it they never can.

The Bible stands and it will forever,
When the world has passed away;
By inspiration it has been given,
All its precepts I will obey.

The Bible stands every test we give it,
For its Author is divine;
By grace alone I will expect to live it,
And to prove it and make it mine.

— HALDOR LILENAS, 1917

THE TRINITY // GOD'S NATURE

> We believe in one God, Creator of all things, holy,
> infinitely perfect, and eternally existing in a loving
> unity of three equally divine Persons: the Father, the
> Son, and the Holy Spirit. Having limitless
> knowledge and sovereign power, God has graciously
> purposed from eternity to redeem a people for
> Himself and to make all things new for His own
> glory.

I f God were small enough to be understood, he wouldn't be big enough to be God.

We believe there is one and only one God. We also believe that our God is united within himself, so that he isn't at all like a bunch of parts rattling around in a box. He is perfectly united and singular and one.

I'm saying all this, because the Trinity is hard to think about. But to grow along the Grace Pathway means we have to stretch our minds around ideas we might have never thought about before.

There is one God, and one nature of God.

At the same time, our one God is three Persons, God the Father, God the Son, and God the Holy Spirit.

The *essence* of God—his nature and being—is always singular and one.

The *Persons* of God—his way of existing—is always plural and triune.

The three persons of the Godhead are co-equal and co-eternal. The Father is fully God, the Son is fully God, and the Holy Spirit is fully God. Everything that God is and everything that God has belongs equally to each person of the Godhead forever. But there is no sense whatsoever in which God is divided, like three different people, or like a beast with three heads. He is One. He is Three.

Mind blown?

Good.

There is nothing in the truth of the Trinity that can possibly be of human origin. Not only are we unlike the Trinity, we find it extremely hard to even imagine such a divine being.

God is not like us.

God is not just a bigger, better version of a human being. Our Triune God is without peer and without parallel.

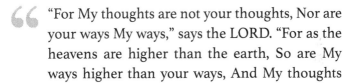 "For My thoughts are not your thoughts, Nor are your ways My ways," says the LORD. "For as the heavens are higher than the earth, So are My ways higher than your ways, And My thoughts than your thoughts." (Isaiah 55:8, 9)

This is super important.

All the gods of all other religions are essentially bigger, better, stronger projections of human nature. But not our God. There is no good comparison to the Trinity.

The people of God would have never in a million years come up with such a teaching. Unless God himself dropped it down from heaven through the inspired writers of Scripture, there would never be any idea of such a being.

To say that the doctrine of the Trinity is hard in no way implies it is irrational. It simply means we are dealing with a transcendent person we can never fully wrap our minds around.

Although the word Trinity is not in the Bible, it doesn't need to be. The teaching echoes across the ages of history and is found throughout the pages of Scripture.

THE SCRIPTURAL CASE FOR THE TRINITY

Jesus teaches, "Go therefore and make disciples of all the nations, baptizing them in the name of the Father and of the Son and of the Holy Spirit..." (Matthew 28:19).

Jesus did not say "names" but "name." In his mind, though God is Three, God is One.

In chapter four, we will look at Scriptures that show that Jesus is God. In chapter five, we will look at Scriptures that show the Holy Spirit is God. This is simply to say that the writers of Scripture saw the Father, Son, and Holy Spirit as equally divine, even as they carefully maintained that there is but one God.

Jesus sang exactly the same tune.

So did the early church leaders. Paul wrote:

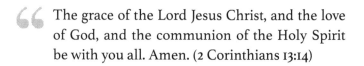 The grace of the Lord Jesus Christ, and the love of God, and the communion of the Holy Spirit be with you all. Amen. (2 Corinthians 13:14)

When a convinced monotheistic Jew like Paul blessed his

friends in the name of the One God, he had no problem referring to his One God in three Persons.

The Old Testament also reflected the Three-in-Oneness of God, though the doctrine is not yet as clear.

For example, the word for God in Hebrew, *Elohim*, is actually a plural noun. But since it's used with singular verbs, even God's name recognizes a plurality of persons within the one God.

The Psalmist writes of God engaging in a conversation within himself — God is talking with God.

The LORD said to my Lord, "Sit at My right hand, Till I make Your enemies Your footstool" (Psalm 110:1).

In fact, the New Testament author of Hebrews makes a collection of Old Testament verses in which God speaks to God to show that the Son of God, Jesus, is fully equal with the Father as God the Son (Hebrews 1:5-13).

This is only an introduction to the vast landscape of biblical teaching on our Triune God.

COMMON MISTAKES

It might be helpful to keep our thinking straight if we briefly look at four common mistakes when it comes to how we think about the Trinity.

1. The mistake of thinking that the Persons of the Trinity take turns.

GOD IS NOT LIKE A SUPERHERO — a mild-mannered geek until he puts on his cape. Some people think that the Father, Son, and Holy Spirit take turns. God is Father for a while, then he runs into the phone booth (do those still exist?) and turns into the Son, until he turns into the Spirit.

If you want to get technical, this mistake is called either Modalism, or Monarchianism (don't blame me, I don't make this stuff up).

This mistake doesn't line up with Scripture. The persons of the Godhead are not "phases." God doesn't just put on different hats.

No.

When Jesus was baptized, all three persons of the Godhead showed their presence at once. The Father was speaking from heaven. The Spirit was descending like a dove. The Son was in the water being baptized.

> When He had been baptized, Jesus came up immediately from the water; and behold, the heavens were opened to Him, and He saw the Spirit of God descending like a dove and alighting upon Him. And suddenly a voice came from heaven, saying, "This is My beloved Son, in whom I am well pleased." (Matthew 3:16, 17)

The three persons of the Godhead are eternal. God is always Father, always Son, and always Holy Spirit.

---

2. The mistake of thinking that the three Persons of the Godhead represent three different pieces of God's nature.

FOR EXAMPLE, some people might say that the Father represents the wrath and transcendence of God, but the Son represents the love and approachability of God, who cajoles the

Father into being nice to us. They might go on to suggest that the Spirit represents the comforting, strengthening aspects of God's presence.

No.

Once again, this mistake fails to honor all that Scripture says about God.

This error, called Sabellianism after an ancient pastor who made it popular, only winds up shrinking God to understandable proportions.

In *Knowing God* (Grace Pathway 3.1), we looked at a handful of attributes of God.

Every person of the Godhead possesses every attribute of God in the fullest possible measure.

The Father is sovereign, the Son is sovereign, the Spirit is sovereign.

The Father is love, the Son is love, the Spirit is love.

Enough said?

When Jesus said, "I and my Father are one," he was claiming to be all that God is, not part of what God is (John 10:30).

---

3. The mistake of thinking that the Father is God, but the Son or the Spirit represent God-lite.

SOME GROUPS SAY that Jesus is God, but they actually want that to be with a little g, god. One ancient teacher said that Jesus was "god", but he was created by the Father, and so less than him. He went on to say that the Spirit was created by Jesus.

No, and no.

This mistake, called Arianism, after Arius, who made it

famous, once again fails to do justice to the Bible.

Scripture is clear:

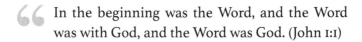 In the beginning was the Word, and the Word was with God, and the Word was God. (John 1:1)

Not some type of junior God. Not some kind of hybrid. Not something less than God.

The father is fully God. Jesus Christ is fully God. The Holy Spirit is fully God. Co-equal. Co-eternal.

---

4. The mistake of confusing the Father with the Son with the Spirit.

GOD THE FATHER did not die on the cross for our sins. It was the Son who went to the Cross.

The Persons of the Godhead might have accepted different roles in our salvation, but they are never to be confused in their person. The Person of the Father is not the Person of the Son is not the Person of the Spirit.

We believe in one God who exists eternally in three distinct persons.

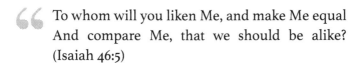 To whom will you liken Me, and make Me equal And compare Me, that we should be alike? (Isaiah 46:5)

GOD IS LOVE

To think of the Trinity is to give new meaning to the truth God is love.

Long before God made anyone or anything, God is love.

In what way? If there was no one else to love, in what way is God love?

The Father loves the Son and the Son loves the Father.

The Son loves the Holy Spirit and the Holy Spirit loves the Son.

The Holy Spirit loves the Father and the Father loves the Holy Spirit.

This love within the Trinity pre-existed everything. From eternity past, the persons of the Godhead shared a closeness and love none of us could ever imagine. The affection, the caring, the delight that each person of the Godhead takes in each other person is a breathtaking mystery beyond comprehension.

For people like us to be brought into that fellowship is a grace we could never fathom (1 John 1:3).

All we can do is bow in wonder, adoration, and praise.

IN THE GREAT and ancient hymn of the church, called the Doxology, the people of God sing:

> *Praise God from whom all blessings flow.*
> *Praise Him all creatures here below.*
> *Praise Him above, ye heav'nly host.*
> *Praise Father, Son, and Holy Ghost.*
> *Amen.*

THE SAVIOR // GOD'S SON

" *We believe that Jesus Christ is God incarnate, fully God and fully man, one Person in two natures. Jesus—Israel's promised Messiah—was conceived through the Holy Spirit and born of the virgin Mary. He lived a sinless life, was crucified under Pontius Pilate, arose bodily from the dead, ascended into heaven and sits at the right hand of God the Father as our High Priest and Advocate.*

Everything in your faith rises and falls on Jesus. Who is he? What do you make of him? What do you do with his claims?

You probably wouldn't have made it this far into the Grace Pathway without having believed in him as your Savior. That moment is like stepping through a doorway into a breathtaking palace. Having Jesus as your Savior first makes it possible to begin experiencing Jesus in all his other titles and roles too.

When we organize all the wonderful truths the Bible tells

us about Jesus, we wind up with two main sub-topics: his Person and his Work.

The Person of Christ tells us who he is and what he is like.

The Work of Christ tells us what he did for us, focused mainly on his saving work in the Cross and Resurrection.

For example, in the doctrinal statement at the beginning of this chapter, there are two sentences. The first sentence talks about the Person of Christ. The second sentence talks about the Work of Christ. Take a look.

In a short chapter like this, we can only study a tiny tip of a gigantic iceberg about the Person and Work of Jesus Christ. The Bible affirms the immensity of his Person and Work:

> And there are also many other things that Jesus did, which if they were written one by one, I suppose that even the world itself could not contain the books that would be written. Amen. (John 21:25)

But it has never been truer of a person to say that to know him is to love him. The more you learn about Jesus, the stronger your love for him will grow. And the stronger your love for him grows, the more you begin to think, believe, live, and choose a life that honors him.

THE PERSON OF CHRIST: FULLY HUMAN / FULLY DIVINE

Just as the Trinity puts God in a class by himself, the Person of Christ puts Jesus in a class by himself too.

Jesus is the only person who pre-existed his own birthday. Long before that first Christmas, long before Joseph and

Mary traveled to Bethlehem, and the Virgin gave birth to a child, the Son of God enjoyed the glories of heaven, since the ages of eternity past.

The first, most important, non-negotiable truth to understand about Jesus is that he is fully human and fully divine. Jesus is the God-Man in ways utterly unlike any of the hybrids of ancient religion.

Jesus is fully God. He is co-equal and co-eternal with God the Father and God the Holy Spirit. He is not a junior god, as we've already seen. Some verses that affirm the deity of Christ include:

- In the beginning was the Word, and the Word was with God, and the Word was God. (John 1:1)
- Jesus said to them, "Most assuredly, I say to you, before Abraham was, I AM." (John 8:58)
- Jesus Christ is the same yesterday, today, and forever. (Hebrews 13:8)

This is not the place to defend doctrine as much as to just lay it out, so I'll not add the overwhelming Scriptural teaching that Jesus Christ is truly, fully, and eternally God Most High. At the same time...

Jesus is fully Human. In his human nature, the only difference between Jesus and everybody else is the complete absence of sin from his life. Jesus lived a perfect and sinless life.

Other than that, he walked the road we all walk. He felt pain. He got tired. He was hungry and thirsty. Jesus wept over things that broke his heart. There were times when he said he didn't know certain things. Whatever limits humans feel, Jesus felt. Whatever pain, whatever temptations, whatever frustrations we feel, Jesus felt to the maximum. He really was a human.

You might wonder how he might feel pain or suffer temptations if he were also God. Couldn't he cheat and use his God powers to make life easier?

Well, he could, but he didn't.

Jesus took it like a man. Though he never laid aside his deity, and he never laid aside his powers, we can say that there were times when Jesus chose not to use powers he always had. In these times, he chose not to use his God-powers, but instead to face life's pains like we do—with human powers only.

For example:

- And the Word became flesh and dwelt among us, and we beheld His glory, the glory as of the only begotten of the Father, full of grace and truth. (John 1:14)
- For there is one God and one Mediator between God and men, the Man Christ Jesus, (1 Timothy 2:5)
- For we do not have a High Priest who cannot sympathize with our weaknesses, but was in all points tempted as we are, yet without sin. (Hebrews 4:15)

Jesus is unique. He is two natures, yet one person. The two natures in Jesus don't blend with each other. He isn't a hybrid like Hercules. His deity remains fully God. His humanity remains fully human. Yet, he is one person, with one mind and one being.

It's another one of those mysteries that makes us understand just how wonderful Jesus is.

THE PERSON OF CHRIST: VIRGIN BORN

Jesus was born of a virgin named Mary. His origin was supernatural.

Because he was born of a virgin, he fulfilled ancient prophecies. For example, eight centuries before he came into the world, the prophet Isaiah wrote:

> "Therefore the Lord Himself will give you a sign: Behold, the virgin shall conceive and bear a Son, and shall call His name Immanuel. (Isaiah 7:14)

When Jesus was born, Matthew wrote:

> So all this was done that it might be fulfilled which was spoken by the Lord through the prophet, saying: "Behold, the virgin shall be with child, and bear a Son, and they shall call His name Immanuel," which is translated, "God with us." (Matthew 1:22, 23)

The virgin birth is important for many reasons.

One of the main reasons is because it reveals the way a person treats the Bible. Do we let the Bible speak for itself, even when what it teaches is hard, or seemingly unscientific, or do we try to cram the Bible into our own grid of presuppositions. Believing in the virgin birth shows that we let the Bible speak for itself, and we accept that with God all things are possible.

The virgin birth is why Jesus was sinless in his human nature. And the virgin birth fulfills the original promise of the gospel, in which the long-awaited Seed of the Woman would crush the head of evil at its source (Genesis 3:15, Galatians 3:16).

There are many other ways to discuss the person of Christ. We can think through his wonderful *names*: Lord, Jesus, Christ, Messiah, Wonderful, Counselor, Mighty God, and over a hundred more.

We can contemplate his numerous *titles*: Mediator, Prophet, Priest, and King.

We can dig into his *attributes*: holiness, love, meekness, courage, power.

Jesus Christ is the most glorious person who has ever graced our dusty planet, and to know him is to love him.

THE WORK OF CHRIST: THE CROSS AND RESURRECTION

When we talk about the Work of Christ, we can talk about a thousand topics.

We can talk about the *life* of Christ, which was sinless, loving, and impactful beyond description.

We can talk about the *teachings* of Christ, which were beautiful, brilliant, eye-opening, and life-giving.

We can talk about the *miracles* of Christ, which pointed to his unique person as the God-man, and demonstrated his mastery over creation.

We can talk about the *character* of Christ, which was without peer in the annals of human heroism.

The work of Christ includes his relationships, travels, integrity, fearlessness, labor, ministry, and carpentry.

But Jesus was more than a carpenter.

And his works were more than a life well-lived.

Everything Jesus said and did was simply a prelude to his

most central work of all.

 For the Son of Man has come to seek and to save that which was lost. (Luke 19:10)

His whole life was a prelude to his death. His life was a qualification and preparation for his death. And it was his death that was his most important work of all.

As we learned in *The Cross* (Grace Pathway 3.2), it was the death of Jesus on the Cross, "crucified under Pontius Pilate" that brought estranged sinners like us back to God.

This was his Prime Directive. The Cross was Christ's Priority One. Paul said, "But God forbid that I should boast except in the cross of our Lord Jesus Christ" (Galatians 6:14).

The Old Rugged Cross is the most precious reality in the hearts and minds of those who deeply love their Savior.

The glorious resurrection of Jesus on the third day was the divine exclamation point to everything Jesus did and said. It was the proof of his Sonship, the doom of the devil, the prototype of life for his people, and the seal of completion on the Father's plan.

Christ is risen!

Christ is risen literally. Christ is risen bodily. Christ is risen personally. Christ is risen eternally. He lives, in his glorified human body, forever.

We believe in an empty tomb, an empty cross, and a Savior whose person and work fills the most important things about our lives.

Thank God for Jesus and his Saving Work.

THE WORK OF CHRIST: PRESENT INTERCESSION

Of all the works Jesus continues today, one of the most precious to us is how he still cares for us from heaven. The Bible paints a beautiful picture of Jesus sitting at the Father's right hand, continually representing us and our needs in heaven.

> Therefore He is also able to save to the uttermost those who come to God through Him, since He always lives to make intercession for them. (Hebrews 7:25)

Jesus is whispering your name to the Father. He claims you as his own, and presents your needs to heaven every single day. This doesn't mean that the Father is hard to please, or that God has forgotten you. No.

It simply means your identity and name is represented in heaven by Jesus your Intercessor. This means your salvation is as secure as Jesus seated on this throne!

God never forgets you. God never neglects you. When you are in trouble, you have "an advocate with the Father, Jesus Christ the righteous" (1 John 2:1).

There has never been, and there will never be, a Savior like Jesus.

One day when Heaven was filled with His praises,
One day when sin was as black as could be,
Jesus came forth to be born of a virgin,
Dwelt among men, my example is He!

Living, He loved me; dying, He saved me;
Buried, He carried my sins far away;
Rising He justified freely forever:
One day He's coming-- O glorious day!

One day they led Him up Calvary's mountain,
One day they nailed Him to die on the tree;
Suffering anguish, despised and rejected:
Bearing our sins, my Redeemer is He!

One day they left Him alone in the garden,
One day He rested, from suffering free;
Angels came down o'er His tomb to keep vigil;
Hope of the hopeless, my Savior is He!

One day the grave could conceal Him no longer,
One day the stone rolled away from the door;
Then He arose, over death He had conquered;
Now is ascended, my Lord evermore!

One day the trumpet will sound for His coming,
One day the skies with His glory will shine;
Wonderful day, my beloved One bringing;
Glorious Savior, this Jesus is mine!

— J. WILBUR CHAPMAN, 1910

THE HOLY SPIRIT // GOD'S REVEALER

> *We believe that the Holy Spirit, in all that He does, glorifies the Lord Jesus Christ. He convicts the world of its guilt. He regenerates sinners, and in Him they are baptized into union with Christ and adopted as heirs in the family of God. He also indwells, illuminates, guides, equips and empowers believers for Christ-like living and service.*

As we have already seen, God is a Trinity. The third person of the Trinity is the Holy Spirit. In some older Bibles, you may sometimes read Holy Ghost, though Spirit is the preferred translation of the underlying Hebrew and Greek words.

The Holy Spirit is God, co-equal and co-eternal with the Father and the Son.

He is not simply an impersonal force. He is not some kind of energy pervading the cosmos. He is not an "it." Nor is he some kind of junior God.

The Holy Spirit is a fully divine person, with all the qualities of divine personhood.

- *The Holy Spirit possesses the divine mind, able to teach God's people:* "But the Helper, the Holy Spirit, whom the Father will send in My name, He will teach you all things, and bring to your remembrance all things that I said to you." (John 14:26)
- *The Holy Spirit possesses the divine will, able to give spiritual gifts to God's people according to his own will:* "But one and the same Spirit works all these things, distributing to each one individually as He wills." (1 Corinthians 12:11)
- *The Holy Spirit possesses divine emotions, able to be grieved and vexed in a uniquely divine way:* "And do not grieve the Holy Spirit of God, by whom you were sealed for the day of redemption." (Ephesians 4:30)

Since the Holy Spirit possesses the divine mind, will, and emotions, he is far more than an impersonal force in the universe.

He is fully God. In fact, Scripture calls him the Lord.

Now the Lord is the Spirit; and where the Spirit of the Lord is, there is liberty. (2 Corinthians 3:17)

It is the Spirit of God who inspired the writers of Scripture:

For prophecy never came by the will of man, but holy men of God spoke as they were moved by the Holy Spirit. (2 Peter 1:21)

This is one reason why Scripture is called "the sword of the Spirit" (Ephesians 6:17).

The Spirit of God brings God's truth to bear on your life, illuminating the gospel and causing you to be saved in the first place. This is why every inch of your Grace Pathway journey is by grace. Your power is never going to be enough for your salvation or life, so God swoops down with his own power in the person of the Spirit.

Here is a quick summary of how God the Holy Spirit works in the life of a believer in Jesus. We'll break it down into the Spirit's pre-salvation, at salvation, and post-salvation ministries.

THE PRE-SALVATION WORK OF THE SPIRIT

1. Convicting of sin

THE FIRST MINISTRY the Holy Spirit did for you personally was to begin convicting you of your sin. Even before you ever realized he was around, it was the Holy Spirit who began poking you, and bugging you, and showing you you needed a Savior. He shows you that the ultimate sin is not believing in Jesus as your Savior.

- And when He has come, He will convict the world of sin, and of righteousness, and of judgment: "of sin, because they do not believe in Me... (John 16:8, 9)

2. Drawing

The second ministry of the Spirit in your life is drawing you to Christ. If you were to look back at all the little things that happened for you to hear about Jesus, that is the Holy Spirit's work. Like a master conductor, he orchestrated the tiniest details of your life so you would come to hear about Jesus.

- The LORD has appeared of old to me, saying: "Yes, I have loved you with an everlasting love; Therefore with lovingkindness I have drawn you." (Jeremiah 31:3)

3. Illuminating the Gospel

In the very moment you are hearing about Jesus, the Holy Spirit is actively helping you understand. The human mind, will, and emotions have been damaged by sin. Our hearts are darkened (Romans 1:21). So the Holy Spirit turns on the lights. Every time anybody hears the good news of Jesus, the Spirit is breaking through the darkness, and shining the light of the gospel of grace. It is the Holy Spirit who, behind the scenes, has led you to the gospel, shows you the gospel, helps you understand the gospel, and enables "whoever wills" to believe the gospel and be saved. It is grace all the way.

- But the natural man does not receive the things of the Spirit of God, for they are foolishness to him; nor can he know them, because they are spiritually discerned. (1 Corinthians 2:14)
- Now we have received, not the spirit of the world, but the Spirit who is from God, that we might

know the things that have been freely given to us
by God. (1 Corinthians 2:12)

THE SALVATION WORK OF THE HOLY SPIRIT

When you heard and believed the gospel, you received Jesus.
He came into you, once for all, and forever. So did the Holy
Spirit. There are three main ways the Holy Spirit blessed you
in the very first nano-second of your salvation.

1. Regeneration

Regeneration, as we saw in *The Cross*, simply means being
born again. It was the Holy Spirit who effected within you
this awesome new birth. It is regeneration that activates all
the indescribable potential you have as a child of God. You
can picture it as God's Spirit moving inside you, and restoring
power to all the circuit breakers that have been turned off.
God's Spirit turns on all the circuits! This is a miracle of
grace.

- "That which is born of the flesh is flesh, and that
  which is born of the Spirit is spirit. . . . The wind
  blows where it wishes, and you hear the sound of
  it, but cannot tell where it comes from and where
  it goes. So is everyone who is born of the Spirit."
  (John 3:6, 8)

2. Baptism into Christ

In the very moment you believe in Jesus, God the Holy
Spirit does something awesome, even though it sounds
weird. He baptizes you into Christ. If you imagine baptism as

plunging into water, you can imagine the Spirit plunging you into Christ. You are in Him. You are joined to him. You are one with Christ forever. This means you share his nature, identity, riches, and destiny, because you've been joined to Jesus. You don't feel this happen, but God says it does, so we believe and move on.

- For by one Spirit we were all baptized into one body—whether Jews or Greeks, whether slaves or free—and have all been made to drink into one Spirit. (1 Corinthians 12:13)
- For as many of you as were baptized into Christ have put on Christ. (Galatians 3:27)

3. Permanent Indwelling

At the moment of faith in Christ, the Spirit of God moves into you. He makes your heart his home. Again, this is nothing you feel or sense, it is simply God's promise being fulfilled. Once he moves in, he will never move out. He will never leave you or forsake you. Once he comes in, it's as if he shuts the door behind him and seals it shut. Having the Spirit of God in you is definitional of being a Christian. This means you never have to ask for God's Spirit. You already have him!

- But you are not in the flesh but in the Spirit, if indeed the Spirit of God dwells in you. Now if anyone does not have the Spirit of Christ, he is not His. (Romans 8:9)
- ...who also has sealed us and given us the Spirit in our hearts as a guarantee. (2 Corinthians 1:22)

THE POST-SALVATION WORK OF THE HOLY SPIRIT

Are you beginning to see the beautiful progression of how God's Spirit works in your life? From beginning to end, the Spirit of God has been working hand in hand with the Father and the Son to bring you to the fullest expression of God's grace and love in your life.

Now that you are saved, the Holy Spirit has several great ministries in your everyday life today. Let's just think about two of them.

1. The Filling of the Holy Spirit

The filling of God's Spirit can sound very mysterious and even spooky to us today. But being filled by the Spirit is the normal way of life for Christians. To be filled with God's Spirit simply means to be *more influenced by the Spirit of God than by other influences in your life.* God's Spirit is leading you to wholeness, beauty, purity, and joy. He is leading you to becoming more and more like Christ in your character and conduct. There are other influences in your life that might be negative, sick, or even evil. When the Holy Spirit influences and guides your life, you will find fulfillment and joy, even in difficult times.

- And do not be drunk with wine, in which is dissipation; but be filled with the Spirit, (Ephesians 5:18)
- And the disciples were filled with joy and with the Holy Spirit. (Acts 13:52)

Some Christians think that being filled with the Spirit involves manifestations such as speaking in tongues other unusual behaviors. This is one of those areas where Christians have a variety of viewpoints. It is best to study these things with your own pastor, church, small group, or fellowship. The main thing the Spirit does is to honor and lift up Jesus Christ. Don't let anything else become the main thing.

- "He [the Spirit] will glorify Me [Jesus Christ], for He will take of what is Mine and declare it to you. (John 16:14)

Let's not confuse the filling of the Spirit with the baptism of the Spirit or the indwelling of the Spirit. The baptism and indwelling of the Holy Spirit are once for all, and forever. But the filling of the Spirit is a repeatable blessing.

The Spirit's baptism and indwelling happen immediately at the moment of your salvation. But the Spirit's filling happens repeatedly after your salvation, as part of your life with God.

So how can you be filled with the Spirit? Jesus said:

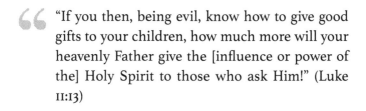

"If you then, being evil, know how to give good gifts to your children, how much more will your heavenly Father give the [influence or power of the] Holy Spirit to those who ask Him!" (Luke 11:13)

If you want to be filled with the Holy Spirit, all you have to do is *ask*. It can be a prayer as simple as, "Dear Lord, please fill me with your Spirit as I go into this meeting. Thank you." Once you *ask*, no matter what you feel or don't feel, *believe* that God has heard you, and that the Spirit has filled you, and get on with your life.

Feelings always take a back seat to faith. As you walk in

the Spirit, the life and character of Christ will be increasingly manifested through you. This is the "manifestation" that counts most!

2. The Fruit of the Holy Spirit

The fruit of the Holy Spirit offers a stark contrast to the "works of the flesh." These works, plural, are nasty. But the Spirit's fruit, singular, like cluster of grapes, is awesome. It is the qualities of Jesus himself being formed in you. As you grow along the Grace Pathway, and as you trust God to fill you with his Spirit, this wonderful fruit develops naturally. It is the outgrowth of the grace of God at work in you.

- But the fruit of the Spirit is love, joy, peace, longsuffering, kindness, goodness, faithfulness, gentleness, self-control. Against such there is no law. (Galatians 5:22, 23)

3. The Comfort, Power, and Help of the Holy Spirit

Jesus promised that he would send his people a Helper. The Greek word here is *parakletos*. Sometimes, especially in older books and hymns, you will find the Spirit called the Paraclete. This word can mean a helper. It can also mean a strengthener and fortifier.

This is how the Holy Spirit operates in your life all the time. He strengthens you (Ephesians 3:16), leads you (Romans 8:14), instructs you as you study God's Word (Nehemiah 9:20), comforts you when you hurt (John 14:26), fills your heart with confidence in God's love, especially as you grow mature on the Grace Pathway (Romans 5:5), and nurtures joy in your life (Acts 13:52).

THE SPIRIT OF GRACE

If you've ever wondered why we call it the Grace Pathway, it is because every single step can only be taken by the grace and power of God.

We don't pay for any of the good things God gives us. They are all paid in full by Jesus already. Thank God for the Cross!

Now do we ourselves energize our forward progress. It's God's Spirit, and therefore his grace, all the way.

One of the titles of the Holy Spirit is "the Spirit of Grace" (Zechariah 12:10, Hebrews 10:29).

He is the Spirit of Grace because he brings the muscle to our lives. Otherwise, we could never be the kind of person we dream of becoming.

 "Not by might nor by power, but by My Spirit,"
Says the LORD of hosts. (Zechariah 4:6)

IF YOU ARE SAVED, you do not have to ask for God's Spirit to come into your life. As we have seen, he already indwells you forever. It is okay, however, to ask for his power and his influence and his filling, believing that he will do so immediately, no matter what you feel.

Hymns such as this one, in which the Holy Spirit is invited to "Come" and "Dwell" are really using that invitation in the sense of his filling, not of his presence (which you already have). This ancient hymn is a beautiful expression of what God's Spirit does when he fills us.

Come, Holy Spirit, come;
Let thy bright beams arise;
Dispel the darkness from our minds,
And open all our eyes.

Cheer our desponding hearts,
Thou heav'nly Paraclete;
Give us to lie with humble hope
At our Redeemer's feet.

Revive our drooping faith;
Our doubts and fears remove;
And kindle in our breasts the flames
Of never-dying love.

Convince us of our sin;
Then lead to Jesus' blood,
And to our wond'ring view, reveal
The secret love of God.

'Tis thine to cleanse the heart,
To sanctify the soul,
To pour fresh life in ev'ry part,
And new create the whole.

Dwell, therefore, in our hearts;
Our minds from bondage free;
Then we shall know and praise and love
The Father, Son, and Thee.

— JOSEPH HART, CA. 1720

CREATION // GOD'S HANDIWORK

> *We believe in one God, the Father, the Almighty,*
> *Maker of heaven and earth, of all that is seen and*
> *unseen.*

— THE NICENE CREED

As we study the basics of our faith along the Grace Pathway, it is important to make sure we are on solid footing. There can be no more solid footing than knowing that the universe and everything in it—including our lives— are the creation of God.

You can look at society as not only a clash of cultures, but also as clash of *stories* about who we are.

I grew up in two worlds—the world of church, and the world of the Chicago public school system.

In the world of church, I learned the story I was created in the image of God.

In the world of the public school system, I learned the story that I evolved from lower forms of life.

My church taught me I was body, soul, and spirit, with a

spark of life lit by the breath of God. The universe was God-centered. It was created by him, and existed for his glory. I had an eternal soul and would live forever, either with or without God.

In my church, I learned all creation was infused with the presence of God, and every day of my life was supercharged with transcendent value.

My school told me a different story. I was a matter and energy molecular machine plus nothing. The universe was an accident, and had no purpose. I was an accident too, bound by time, and when my chemical machine wore out, I snuffed out like a candle, and that was it. There was nothing after death.

In my school, I learned that the space-time continuum was all there is, and every day of life was defined by the survival of the fittest.

The world of church lifted the veil of existence and showed me the face of a Creator God upholding and redeeming all things. It taught me a story in which I am the epitome of creation.

The world of school showed me a mechanical universe with no soul. I am the product of evolution.[1]

The message of creation resounds from Scripture with undeniable power and logic.

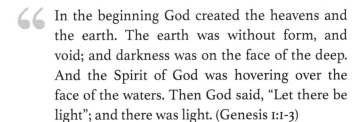 In the beginning God created the heavens and the earth. The earth was without form, and void; and darkness was on the face of the deep. And the Spirit of God was hovering over the face of the waters. Then God said, "Let there be light"; and there was light. (Genesis 1:1-3)

The whole creation tells of the majesty of God. It is a

testament to his creative power and genius, a monument to his love. Whether the beauty of a flower, or the wonders of a baby's hand, or the glories a vast cosmos, all-that-is testifies to an Infinite God whose mind imagined and whose hand created all things.

While Christians may hold a variety of viewpoints as to the precise dating and methodology by which God created all things and outfitted earth for our habitation, all Bible-believing Christians see the cosmos as sitting in the hand of the God who made it.

"He's got the whole wide world in his hands..."

The issue is bigger than creation alone. Your view on creation reveals something deeper about you. Will you submit your beliefs and life to the authority of God's Word or not? Where will you find your truth?

If you find your truth in the Bible, you will discover the wonderful blessings of a universe created by God from nothing.

There are plenty of excellent apologetics-type books that demonstrate the truthfulness of the Genesis account. This is not a book on apologetics, so I will save some of that discussion for book 4.3 in the Grace Pathway. However, we can think together about three essential truths flowing out from the doctrine of God's creation.

DIVINE CREATION MAKES MORALITY POSSIBLE

If you dig through the layers of existence only to find randomness at the core—as secular materialists say—you will find no objective basis for right and wrong. If the universe is the product of blind forces, or if life is the product of chance, then morality is equally blind and random.

This is because we cannot be held accountable for our moral choices. For materialists, who define the cosmos in terms of matter and energy, free will is an illusion. Everything is pre-determined by cause and effect, matter and energy. Albert Einstein voiced this all-too-common conclusion, "human beings in their thinking, feeling, and acting, are not free but are as causally bound as the stars in their motions."[2]

If we are not free, and if we are "causally bound" in our moral choices, then why should anybody be held accountable for their actions?

The logic is flawless. To subtract God is to subtract free will. To subtract free will is to erase any objective basis for morality. Right and wrong become nothing but social constructs. When society cannot agree on moral issues, it becomes a tug of war, where "might makes right."

On the Postmodern side, those who admit a deity, but then define it in impersonal terms (pantheism) or as pagan pantheons (Zeus, Hercules, Athena, Odin, Freya, Thor), find the same dilemma. By what standard can we judge right and wrong if the gods themselves have no standards or are fickle in upholding them?

If you cannot judge between good and evil, you have no basis for fighting evil. You have no basis to even criticize evil. It's just the *Lord of the Flies* and survival of the fittest all the time.

But if there is a God as described in Scripture, and if he has spoken, then there is an objective right and wrong. His laws —moral laws as well as physical laws—govern all of existence.

God's laws are not arbitrary. He did not "make them up." Rather, God's moral laws flow out of his heart. God's laws are

God's laws because God's heart is God's heart. Since his heart overflows with love, his law is not merely a code of ethics, but a revelation of love.

 Owe no one anything except to love one another, for he who loves another has fulfilled the law. (Romans 13:8)

This is why no one can break God's laws. We can only break ourselves against God's laws. It is also why we need a Savior, and why we are so thankful for his grace.

Any worldview that denies the Creator inevitably erases morality and dehumanizes society. What other result can there be from trampling the Law of Love?

Without a divine Creator, our moral code can only echo a somber ancient warning: "In those days there was no king in Israel; everyone did what was right in his own eyes" (Judges 17:6).

DIVINE CREATION GIVES MAXIMUM DIGNITY TO HUMANKIND

Ideas have consequences. Once you erase the biblical idea of humans created in the image of God, you turn us into nothing more than animals. We do not bear the divine spark of life, so we are simply the best that evolution can do for now.

If we are simply animals, then who's to say we're more valuable than any other animal? Aren't humans just highly evolved livestock, valued by our "contribution" to the general welfare? And, as livestock, can't we just do away with the weak, the infirm, the disabled, the elderly, the pre-born, the newly born, or the simply "undesirable"?

Without creation in the image of God, our value is extrinsic, not intrinsic.

In an article entitled "A Rat Is a Pig Is a Dog Is a Boy," Ingrid Newkirk directly equates animal life with human life. There is no difference in value or worth between a rat and a boy or girl.[3] This radical devaluation of human life yields consequences that are playing out in our fragmented and violent cultures of today.

To devalue the sanctity of human life is to murder the quality called love.

It is the Judeo-Christian heritage, standing on the revealed Word of God and the doctrine of Creation, that makes human life sacred. Humans are special to God in ways that no other life-forms are special.

 Then God said, "Let Us make man in Our image, according to Our likeness; let them have dominion over the fish of the sea, over the birds of the air, and over the cattle, over all the earth and over every creeping thing that creeps on the earth." So God created man in His own image; in the image of God He created him; male and female He created them. Then God blessed them, and God said to them, "Be fruitful and multiply; fill the earth and subdue it; have dominion over the fish of the sea, over the birds of the air, and over every living thing that moves on the earth." (Genesis 1:26-28)

We bear the divine image. We carry certain elements, in finite fashion, of the very nature of infinite God. We have eternal souls and spirits. We have a special relationship with God. We have moral obligations not incumbent on other creatures. We will live forever, one way or another.

Human life is sacred. Human beings are precious. We were created for dignity, respect, and honor. We are the pinnacle of God's craftsmanship. We belong to God, and no one has the right to harm, devalue, exploit, or own us in any way.

> What is man that You are mindful of him, And the son of man that You visit him? For You have made him a little lower than the angels, And You have crowned him with glory and honor. (Psalms 8:4, 5)

We are a little lower than angels in our present power and visible glory, but a day is coming when…

> Therefore God also has highly exalted Him and given Him the name which is above every name, that at the name of Jesus every knee should bow, of those in heaven, and of those on earth, and of those under the earth, and that every tongue should confess that Jesus Christ is Lord, to the glory of God the Father. (Philippians 2:9-11)

When the angels bow to Jesus, they will bow to us, in Him. We are "crowned with glory and honor," ultimately, even above angels.

Our origin possesses a glory that can be bestowed neither by evolution nor by the creation-myths of history. Our destiny, therefore possesses a potential glory that far transcends even the most utopian, evolutionary sci-fi imaginings.

It is the biblical account of creation alone that elevates the dignity and worth of every human, from conception onward, to levels our minds can barely comprehend.

DIVINE CREATION ACCOUNTS FOR SPIRITUAL REALITIES

A worldview provides a mental map for your life. As you develop your worldview, you piece together experiences and life-lessons into a singular whole. You are trying to understand, and to give meaning, to everything you discover along life's journey.

This is your worldview.

Problems come, however, when your worldview draws a map too small for your experiences.

For example, atheistic evolutionary theory draws a map that does not allow for a truly human mind, for free will, or for objective morality.

But experience contradicts those conclusions every single day. So does logic. If you are truly logical, and truly scientific (empirical, experiential), then you will fall off the edge of your map every time you feel an emotion, have an opinion, make a choice, or love somebody.

J. Richard Pearcey notes, "Materialists thereby deny the reality of mind (while they use their minds to advance materialism), determinists deny the reality of human choice (while they choose determinism), and relativists deny the fact of right and wrong (while they judge you if you disagree)."[4]

They are falling off their own maps.

When experience contradicts your worldview, do you explain away your experience, or do you adjust your worldview?

This is, in some ways, the greatest question of your life.

It is the story of divine creation alone, as revealed in the Bible, that draws a map big enough that we don't fall off it. No philosophy, no revelation, no religion, no scientific viewpoint, and no other system of thought can account for everything we experience, think, imagine, feel, and know to be true, as well as the biblical worldview.

You will never fall off the edge of the Bible's map of reality.

These basic doctrines we are thinking about in this book describe the actual, experiential, demonstrable contours of our lives and our worlds.

Is there love in your life? That fits on the Bible's map of truth. Are you free to make choices? That also fits on the Bible's map. Is there a vast universe of mind-boggling scope? Is there matter? Is there energy? Is there a macro-world that must be accounted for? Is there a micro-world too complex to have made itself? Is the universe imbued with the majesties and glories of a Designer? Are there scientific laws that govern nature? Do the birds and trees and sun and moon testify of a Creator? Are there transcendent values of the human heart? Are some things right and some things wrong? Are some things true and some things false? Is there a singular truth, a unified reality, at the core of everything? Does life have meaning and purpose? Are humans of measureless worth? Are we free? Is love real, truth real, and hope real?

All the realities of life fit squarely, and uniquely, on the map drawn by Scripture. No other worldview can account for it all. None. You'll never find one.

> — ALL THE REALITIES OF LIFE FIT SQUARELY ON THE MAP DRAWN BY THE AUTHOR OF THE AUTHORS OF SCRIPTURE.

That is why *"We believe in one God, the Father, the Almighty, Maker of heaven and earth, of all that is seen and unseen."*

And that is why we take our stand on the most transcendent, life-affirming, yet simple sentence ever put together: "In the beginning, God created the heavens and the earth."

O Lord my God, when I in awesome wonder
Consider all the *worlds thy hands have made,
I see the stars, I hear the *rolling thunder,
Thy power throughout the universe displayed:

Then sings my soul, my Savior God, to thee:
How great thou art! How great thou art!
Then sings my soul, my Savior God, to thee:
How great thou art! How great thou art!

When through the woods and forest glades I
    wander
And hear the birds sing sweetly in the trees,
When I look down from lofty mountain grandeur,
And hear the brook and feel the gentle breeze:

And when I think that God, his Son not sparing,
Sent him to die, I scarce can take it in,
That on the cross, my burden gladly bearing,
He bled and died to take away my sin.

When Christ shall come with shout of acclamation
And take me home, what joy shall fill my heart!
Then I shall bow in humble adoration,
And there proclaim, "My God, how great thou art!"

— ATTRIBUTED TO STUART K. HINE,

1920

---

1. Some of this introductory material is adapted from one of my apologetics books, *Illusions* (Endurant Press, 2018, chapter 6).
2. Cited in Pearcey, Nancy. *Finding Truth: 5 Principles for Unmasking Atheism, Secularism, and Other God Substitutes* (p. 158). David C Cook. Kindle Edition.
3. Ingrid Newkirk, "A Rat Is a Pig Is a Dog Is a Boy" from PETA's website, last updated March 6, 2015, at https://www.peta.org/blog/rat-pig-dog-boy/ retrieved July 31, 2019.
4. In Nancy Pearcey. *Finding Truth: 5 Principles for Unmasking Atheism, Secularism, and Other God Substitutes* (p. 19). David C Cook. Kindle Edition.

HUMANKIND // GOD'S IMAGE

> *We believe that God created Adam and Eve in His image, but they sinned when tempted by Satan. In union with Adam, human beings are sinners by nature and by choice, alienated from God, and under His wrath. Only through God's saving work in Jesus Christ can we be rescued, reconciled and renewed.*

The story the Bible tells of humankind rings true to experience. This story is the exact opposite of the story being told by the spirit of the age, by the philosophies of the world, and by the presuppositions of non-objective science.

One story says humans are evolving. We are improving physiologically, intellectually. We are even improving morally. The human race is ascending. This is the spirit of evolution.

But the Bible's story smashes that story in the face. Not evolution, but devolution. We are not stepping up. What we are today is a massive step down from what we once were.

Which story rings true to experience? Which story better

explains the world? Your world? Does history show us being less brutal?

No.

Technology has improved, but we are the same brutes we've been since the Fall revealed in Genesis 3. Thank God for the redeeming grace of the Cross.

ADAM AND EVE

The original parents of our race were created by the hand of God. Adam and Eve were utterly perfect. They possessed the unlimited capacities of a perfect and true human nature. Having been created in God's image, they were sacred to God in ways unlike any other being.

> And the LORD God formed man of the dust of the ground, and breathed into his nostrils the breath of life; and man became a living being. (Genesis 2:7)

They were real. They were ideal.

As humans, Adam and Eve possessed a body, soul, and spirit.

Their bodies were perfect.

No pains, no diseases, no process of death was at work in them. Whatever is the ideal age for a human, that's how old they were. They were healthy, vibrant, and strong. They didn't need glasses. They didn't lose any hair. They didn't need pain-killers. Their bodies were formed by the hand of

God with utter and complete perfection. Physically, Adam and Eve could live indefinitely, without ever showing signs of age.

Their souls were perfect.

Consisting of mind, will, and emotions, their souls possessed astounding capacities. Their minds were completely awake, functional, and of mega-genius I.Q. Their wills were completely and utterly free, with no internal temptation to sin. Their emotions were pure joy and boundless love. No sadness, no depression, no neediness, and no dysfunction marred their inner worlds.

Their spirits were perfect.

The spirit is the part of a human that interfaces with God. God's Spirit connects with our human spirit. Every day, Adam and Eve enjoyed the company of God in the Garden of Eden. He walked and talked with them "in the cool of the day" (Genesis 3:8). There was nothing between them and God.

Perfect in body, soul, and spirit. Dwelling in the perfect environment of the Garden of Eden. This is the profile of Adam and Eve before the terrible, horrible, no good, every bad day called the Fall.

THE FALL

Everything changed the day Adam and Eve invited sin into the world.

Adam's Original Sin infected us all.

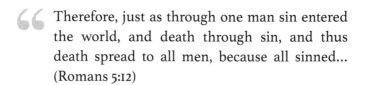

> Therefore, just as through one man sin entered the world, and death through sin, and thus death spread to all men, because all sinned... (Romans 5:12)

All sinned when Adam sinned, that's the idea. We were in him. We were part of him. The whole human race was knocked down by the original sin.

Not only did they invite sin into the world, they invited death too. God had warned them:

"but of the tree of the knowledge of good and evil you shall not eat, for in the day that you eat of it you shall surely die" (Genesis 2:17).

Their spirits died immediately.

Adam and Eve lost their wonderful relationship with God. They hid from him. They felt shame before him. For the first time, they felt naked and vulnerable before God.

Their soul began the process of death.

Their minds were clouded, and they lost most of their intellectual capacity. Their emotions were darkened, and for the first time they felt sadness, fear, and shame. Their wills were distorted, and they felt an inner pull toward sin. In their deepest personality, Adam and Eve felt estranged from God. They covered themselves and hid from him (Genesis 3:7, 8). This is part of the death they died that day.

Their bodies began the processes of decay, disease, and death.

Death didn't just enter the world that day, it entered their bodies. This was the first human experience of pain, of aging, of the breakdown of the body. Eyes would go. Joints would go. Memories would go. Hair would go. The human body would break down and one day die.

Adam and Eve were sinners by choice.

But something deeper happened that day. They were changed—body, soul, and spirit. Something broke in them, in each element of their being.

They were not only sinners by choice.

They were now sinners by nature, too.

But it gets worse. Because they were sinners by nature and by choice, they were also deemed sinful by the Supreme Court of heaven.

OUR DOUBLE PROBLEM

Theology experts put it this way. Sin caused a double-problem for us.

- Because of the Fall, Adam and Eve felt the *corruption* of sin in their essence and being.
- Because of the Fall, Adam and Eve felt the *guilt* of sin in their standing before God.

Corruption and guilt.

This was the moral profile of Adam and Eve the nano-second after they sinned. This is the profile of spiritual death.

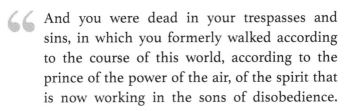

> And you were dead in your trespasses and sins, in which you formerly walked according to the course of this world, according to the prince of the power of the air, of the spirit that is now working in the sons of disobedience.

Among them we too all formerly lived in the lusts of our flesh, indulging the desires of the flesh and of the mind, and were by nature children of wrath, even as the rest. (Ephesians 2:1-3, NASB)

Every human being born into the world bears this exact profile of corruption and guilt. This is what is meant by Original Sin.

— EVERY HUMAN BEING BORN INTO THE WORLD BEARS THIS EXACT PROFILE OF CORRUPTION AND GUILT.

Original Sin means we all come into the world as moral duplicates of our fallen father Adam. We are spiritually dead and under divine judgment.

We are sinners by nature. Every last one of us. The best of us. The worst of us. And we all prove it on the day we're old enough to become sinners by choice. There's an old saying that says we're not sinners because we have sinned; we have sinned because we are sinners.

...For there is no difference; for all have sinned and fall short of the glory of God, (Romans 3:22, 23)

Sin wiped us all out. It was the great equalizer—there is no difference between us in our internal corruption of guilt. On the surface level, some sinners seem worse than others. But on the inside, we're all the same.

We are fallen members of a fallen race. We are alienated

from God (Ephesians 4:8, Colossians 1:21). We are deserving of, and under the wrath of, God (Romans 1:18).

This is the birth of all suffering. This is the reason why we hurt each other. This is the reason why God seems so far away. And this is the reason why we so desperately need a Savior.

All of the problems we discussed in The Cross (Grace Pathway Milestone 3.2) have their birth right here. Sin, the Penalty of Sin, No Righteousness, our maladjustment to the Holiness of God, Spiritual Death, and Spiritual Bondage. The day Adam sinned, their humanly irreconcilable problems popped into existence. All the pieces of theology fit perfectly together into a matchless tapestry of divine truth.

ARE HUMANS BASICALLY GOOD?

Are humans basically good?

The short answer is, "Not any more."

We were created good. But since the Fall, our nature has become sinful. This does not erase our ability to do good. This does not deny the nobility humans often show. All of these beautiful things demonstrate that the image of God has not been erased from our being.

But sin has so overwhelmed who and what we are, that we can never fix ourselves. We are sinners. All of us. Equally. "For there is no difference, for all have sinned... (Romans 3:22b, 23).

Think carefully before you push back against this bad news. Jesus didn't come to save righteous people. He came to save sinners. He said so (Mark 2:17, cf., 1 Timothy 1:15).

Don't worry, you qualify.

So in comes the good news of God. Just as God himself performed the first sacrifice to cover Adam and Eve in coats of skin, so he also performed the ultimate Sacrifice on Calvary's hill.

> For scarcely for a righteous man will one die; yet perhaps for a good man someone would even dare to die. But God demonstrates His own love toward us, in that while we were still sinners, Christ died for us. (Romans 5:7, 8)

In the next chapter, we will go deeper into God's mind-boggling plan to turn Sinners into Saints.

THIS CLASSIC HYMN, composed in 1776 by Augustus Toplady, reveals a deep understanding of the fallen human condition. Notice how the first verse points to the Cross as sin's "double cure."

The first cure is to save us from "wrath," which is the consequence of our *guilt*.

The second cure is to "make me pure," which is the process by which God delivers us from *corruption*. We will find out about this in the next chapter.

If you know the melody, sing along. If you don't, you can still appreciate the depth of meaning woven into beautiful poetry.

> *Rock of Ages, cleft for me,*
> *Let me hide myself in thee;*
> *Let the water and the blood,*
> *From thy wounded side which flowed,*
> *Be of sin the double cure;*
> *Save from wrath and make me pure.*

Not the labors of my hands
Can fulfill thy law's demands;
Could my zeal no respite know,
Could my tears forever flow,
All for sin could not atone;
Thou must save, and thou alone.

Nothing in my hand I bring,
Simply to the cross I cling;
Naked, come to thee for dress;
Helpless, look to thee for grace;
Foul, I to the fountain fly;
Wash me, Savior, or I die.

While I draw this fleeting breath,
When mine eyes shall close in death,
When I soar to worlds unknown,
See thee on thy judgment throne,
Rock of Ages, cleft for me,
Let me hide myself in thee.

— AUGUSTUS TOPLADY,

1776

SALVATION // GOD'S GIFT

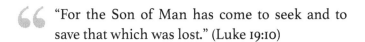 *We believe that Jesus Christ, as our representative and substitute, shed His blood on the cross as the perfect, all-sufficient sacrifice for our sins. His atoning death and victorious resurrection constitute the only ground for salvation.*

J esus came to save. That was his main thing. Nobody understands Christianity without not only understanding salvation, but receiving it too.

Any group or denomination or church or preacher that does not communicate and prioritize salvation is missing the main reason Jesus came.

"For the Son of Man has come to seek and to save that which was lost." (Luke 19:10)

Salvation is non-negotiable. It is definitional of being a Christian. There is no such thing as a Christian who has not yet been saved! Salvation is a clear dividing line.

It is not optional.

Jesus said, "You must be born again" (John 3:7).

Peter said, "We must be saved" (Acts 4:12).

Paul said, "Now if anyone does not have the Spirit of Christ, he is not His" (Romans 8:9).

Christianity is not like a coat you pull on top of your clothes. It is a radical transformation of your status and being. You literally become "a new creation" (2 Corinthians 5:17). In your relationship with God, there is nothing more important than salvation (Galatians 6:15).

Of all the big deals in your life, salvation is by far the biggest deal of all.

WHAT IS SALVATION?

Salvation is the free gift of God, based on the sacrifice of Christ, by which God welcomes an undeserving sinner, now called a saint, into his family forever through faith alone in Christ alone.

> — SALVATION IS THE FREE GIFT OF GOD, BASED ON THE SACRIFICE OF CHRIST, BY WHICH GOD WELCOMES AN UNDESERVING SINNER, NOW CALLED A SAINT, INTO HIS FAMILY FOREVER THROUGH FAITH ALONE IN CHRIST ALONE.

1. Salvation is Step One.

The Grace Pathway begins with "God Saves You." That's the first step. God cannot bless you, grow you, or use you until you are saved.

If life with God is a palace, then salvation is the threshold. It is an absolute dividing line. You have either stepped across the threshold or not. In or out.

Every person is either saved or not saved. There are no gray areas here.

This is not a matter of getting involved in a church or being a good person. It is completely about what you have done with Jesus Christ.

Who is Jesus to you?

Where is your hope for eternity?

Is Jesus part of your trust or is he all?

Are you saved?

2. Salvation is pure grace.

There is no part of salvation that we earn. No part that we deserve. No part that we merit. No part that we pay for. All the burden rests on God's shoulders. All the cost is paid by him. Salvation is one hundred percent grace. The biggest mistake anyone can ever make is to add costs, conditions, and fine print to the wonderful gift of salvation.

> For by grace you have been saved through faith, and that not of yourselves; it is the gift of God, not of works, lest anyone should boast. (Ephesians 2:8, 9)

A free gift is a free gift.

Our job is to guard the gospel from all sorts of legalistic (duty-based) additions.

It is a gigantic mistake to load people with duties and obligations they simply cannot bear. What a tragedy when church people turn the good news of an utterly free gift into the bad news of sweating for a paycheck!

Jesus is no partial Savior. He doesn't save us halfway, and demand we meet him in the middle. No. Jesus did all the saving work, and when we say yes, God saves us once for all and forever.

3. Salvation is eternal.

Salvation was a gift conceived and designed in eternity past by our Triune God. The Father authored the plan, the Son implemented the plan, and the Spirit reveals and applies the plan to the human heart.

Jesus was the Lamb of God, "slain from the foundation of the world" (Revelation 13:8).

When a person is saved, they immediately receive eternal life.

> And this is the testimony: that God has given us eternal life, and this life is in His Son. He who has the Son has life; he who does not have the Son of God does not have life. (1 John 5:11, 12)

Let that sink in. If you have the Son, you have eternal life. Already.

Eternal life doesn't begin when you die. It begins the moment you receive Jesus as your Savior! We could say that your salvation was the day when your clock *stopped* ticking, forever.

4. Salvation is complete from the moment you first believe.

You don't grow into your possession of salvation. You

receive the whole thing all at once. This happens in the first nano-second you believe.

Nobody is "kind-of" saved.

God isn't meting out his gift bit by bit. You get the whole spectacular thing all at once.

The Barrier is demolished, the veil is torn down the middle, and you are reconciled to God. Christ's work on the Cross made this possible.

God isn't holding out on you. He isn't waiting for you to prove yourself before he "finalizes" your salvation. You are as fully saved on day one as you will ever be.

You are "complete in Him" the Bible says, because your salvation is perfect from beginning to end (Colossians 2:10).

5. Salvation affects you in three tenses.

Eternity resides in your heart, but your body, soul, and spirit are still crawling through time, along with everybody else. The wonders of salvation unfold in your life, day by day, as time goes on. That is why the Scriptures speak of salvation in three tenses—past, present, and future.

Past Tense - Saved from the *Penalty* of Sin

When the Bible speaks of salvation as a done deal, it is referring to complete salvation from the penalty of sin forever. "For by grace you have been saved..." in the past tense with results that continue forever (Ephesians 2:8).

There is no punishment, no condemnation, no judgment, and no penalty that was not absorbed, felt, and paid in full in Jesus Christ as he died on the Cross. Since he bore the full weight of the penalty of sin, your past-tense salvation has been completed forever.

In this past tense aspect, salvation is instantaneous. It flips a switch that can never be unflipped.

You are washed clean, you are forgiven, you are accepted, you are adopted, you are joined to Christ, and on and on. All of the incredible blessings of salvation are yours because you have been placed in Christ at the first moment you believed.

This past tense aspect of salvation is what most people think of when they think of salvation.

But the past tense reality of salvation in your life generates a present tense reality too.

Present Tense - Saved from the *Power* of Sin

Sometimes the Bible speaks of our salvation in the present tense. Salvation isn't just our history, it's our everyday life as well.

While the past tense aspect of salvation is instantaneous, this present tense aspect is progressive. It unfolds over time.

What is God doing through our present tense salvation?

God is empowering us to follow Jesus in our thoughts, words, and actions. With this power, we can rise above temptation. With this power, we can display the love of Jesus to people around us. With this power, we can develop the character of Christ.

This present tense aspect of salvation has a theological name. It is called Sanctification — the process by which God makes a person holy (whole, wholesome) in their everyday life.

It is also called your Christian life or your Christian "walk." The Bible explains we are saved in the past tense that we might "walk in newness of life" in the present tense (Romans 6:4).

Notice the present tense in this verse:

> For the message of the cross is foolishness to those who are perishing, but to us who are being saved it is the power of God. (1 Corinthians 1:18)

If you were saved in the past, you also, by definition "are being saved" in the present. This simply means that the power and influence of God are always present in your life.

We will learn more about this awesome present tense work of salvation both in chapter 10, and we'll go into even more depth when we reach Grace Pathway Milestone 4.

Future Tense - Saved from the *Presence* of Sin

One day, Jesus will return. It will be a glorious moment. When you finally see him face to face, you will experience the future tense aspect of salvation.

On that day, sin will be totally erased from your life. No more temptation. No more struggles to be holy. No more bad habits. No more addiction, self-pity, selfishness, or pride.

All that bad stuff is wiped out by the personal presence of Jesus Christ.

All this will happen instantaneously, when Christ appears (more on this in chapter 12).

Even the damaging effects of sin in your body will be gone. No more pain. No more aching joints. No more foggy memories. No more process of death. Salvation will be complete, and sin will be history.

> For our citizenship is in heaven, from which we also eagerly wait for the Savior, the Lord Jesus Christ, who will transform our lowly body that

it may be conformed to His glorious body, according to the working by which He is able even to subdue all things to Himself. (Philippians 3:20, 21)

A KNOW-SO PROPOSITION

As Christians, we have the incredible blessing of knowing for sure we are saved. We can say, "I know I belong to Jesus. I know my sins are forgiven. I know I am going to heaven some day. I know I belong to God and he belongs to me forever."

This is not arrogance. After all, we didn't save ourselves.

This is faith.

This is confidence in the saving work of God and reliance on the finished work of Christ. This breathtaking confidence is encouraged in Scripture.

Salvation is not a hope-so proposition. I'm not keeping my fingers crossed and hoping for the best when I die.

Salvation is a know-so proposition. I'm saved and I know it. All because of Christ. He is my hope, all my hope, and my only hope.

There is no Plan B. We don't need a Plan B. If you have Jesus, you are saved forever. In him, you have all you need.

 These things I have written to you who believe in the name of the Son of God, that you may know that you have eternal life, and that you may continue to believe in the name of the Son of God. (1 John 5:13)

THERE ARE SO many wonderful hymns of salvation, but this one is so rich in doctrine, I just had to include it.

Saved by the blood of the Crucified One!
Now ransomed from sin and a new work begun,
Sing praise to the Father and praise to the Son,
Saved by the blood of the Crucified One!

Glory, I'm saved! glory, I'm saved!
My sins are all pardoned, my guilt is all gone!
Glory, I'm saved! glory, I'm saved!
I'm saved by the blood of the Crucified One!

Saved by the blood of the Crucified One!
The angels rejoicing because it is done;
A child of the Father, joint heir with the Son,
Saved by the blood of the Crucified One!

Saved by the blood of the Crucified One!
The Father—He spake, and His will—it was done;
Great price of my pardon, His own precious Son;
Saved by the blood of the Crucified One!

Saved by the blood of the Crucified One!
All hail to the Father, all hail to the Son,
All hail to the Spirit, the great Three in One!
Saved by the blood of the Crucified One!

— S. J. HENDERSON, 1902

THE CHURCH // GOD'S FAMILY

> *We believe that the true church comprises all who have been justified by God's grace through faith alone in Christ alone. They are united by the Holy Spirit in the body of Christ, of which He is the Head. The true church is manifest in local churches, whose membership should be composed only of believers. The Lord Jesus mandated two ordinances, baptism and the Lord's Supper, which visibly and tangibly express the gospel. Though they are not the means of salvation, when celebrated by the church in genuine faith, these ordinances confirm and nourish the believer.*

If Jesus is the hope of the world, then the Church is the dispenser of that hope. Since the church is made up of people, however, we dispense that hope imperfectly.

Many people criticize the church—in many cases, rightly so.

But God loves the Church. To God, the church is beautiful, even with her imperfections. She is the Bride of Christ and the Body of Christ (Ephesians 5:26,27 and 1 Corinthians 12:27). God is always working on his church that he might work through the church to summon a lost world to himself.

Jesus said,

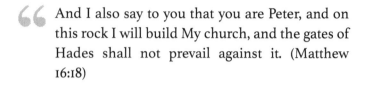

> And I also say to you that you are Peter, and on this rock I will build My church, and the gates of Hades shall not prevail against it. (Matthew 16:18)

Peter, whose name means "little rock," has just confessed that Jesus is the "Messiah, the Son of the Living God" (v. 17). This confession is the rock—the giant boulder—on which Jesus will build his church.

WHAT IS THE CHURCH?

When we think of the Church, the first thing we have to do is separate the idea of the church from its buildings. The place and buildings do not make up the church.

The people make up the church.

In fact, the New Testament word for church is *ecclesia*, which gives us words like ecclesiastical, and ecclesiology. *Ecclesia* means "called out." Christians are people who have been called out from the world and into the family of God.

That is why we think of the church in two main ways: the Universal Church and the local church.

The Universal Church

The Universal Church is made up of all believers in Jesus Christ, past, present, and future, living and dead, wherever they may be in creation. This is sometimes called the Invisible Church or simply the Church.

All people who confess Jesus Christ as their Savior are part of this one, holy, universal, and apostolic—meaning resting on the biblical teaching of the early apostles—church.

 > For by one Spirit we were all baptized into one
> body--whether Jews or Greeks, whether slaves
> or free--and have all been made to drink into
> one Spirit. (1 Corinthians 12:13)

It's incredible to think that we are one in spirit with believers on other continents, in other socio-economic groups, who speak other languages, and express their faith within other cultures, than our own. We are even one in spirit with those who have already gone to heaven!

This is the marvelous diversity of the body of Christ. We are brothers and sisters with believers from every tongue and tribe and nation around the world and across the millennia.

The devil is afraid of the Universal Church. He resists it with all his might.

The Local Church

The Local Church is made up of believers in Jesus who gather regularly to worship God, grow in grace, and be equipped to serve him in the world.

Local churches are the churches that will gather in buildings on street corners and in homes and shops. There is a huge variety of expression from church to church.

There are literally thousands of denominations, which are basically families of local churches.

Sometimes, these denominations form because of differences in doctrine. Most of those differences are slight, though some can be fairly major. That's why it's important to nail down the basics, and to gather with a church that holds fast to God's Word.

Other times, these denominations form because of differences, not in doctrine, but in methodology—what kind of music to use in worship, what kind of evangelistic techniques are used, how liturgical to be, what styles of clothing, speech, language shall we express.

Yet other times, these denominations form because of differences in how they define their mission—denominations are formed to reach urban, suburban, or rural people, this language group or that language group, or this region or that region.

All of this variety is beautiful and is essential for the mission of evangelism.

When local churches divided for healthy reasons—to provide a variety in how we reach the world for Christ, and to better saturate different regions or people groups with the gospel—we celebrate our differences.

When the church is divided for unhealthy reasons, such as doctrinal error, or bigotry, it breaks our hearts.

In all cases, we remember the Universal Church, which joins us all as one in Christ, as the backdrop to the myriads of local church gatherings throughout the world. Wherever Jesus Christ—the God-man, crucified, risen again, the world's only Savior—is believed and the Word of God is proclaimed, and the people of God are reaching out to lost people with the gospel, God is pleased.

 What then? Only that in every way, whether in pretense or in truth, Christ is preached; and in this I rejoice, yes, and will rejoice. (Philippians 1:18)

The two most important things are truth and love. We love one another in spite of our differences. And we are always opening our Bibles, and striving to accurately reflect the truth God has revealed in his Word.

The church is messy because the church is people and people are messy. Don't worry, you'll fit right in.

Every believer in Jesus is called to be an integral part of a local church. Your participation in a local church is both a cause of, and an expression of, your growth in maturity along the Grace Pathway.

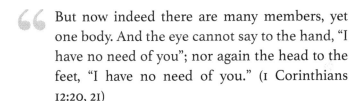

But now indeed there are many members, yet one body. And the eye cannot say to the hand, "I have no need of you"; nor again the head to the feet, "I have no need of you." (1 Corinthians 12:20, 21)

THE MISSION OF THE CHURCH

Jesus was very clear about the mission of his church. He gave his early church leaders, called apostles, their marching orders.

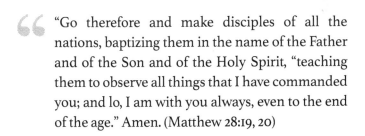

"Go therefore and make disciples of all the nations, baptizing them in the name of the Father and of the Son and of the Holy Spirit, "teaching them to observe all things that I have commanded you; and lo, I am with you always, even to the end of the age." Amen. (Matthew 28:19, 20)

"But you shall receive power when the Holy Spirit has come upon you; and you shall be witnesses to Me in Jerusalem, and in all Judea and Samaria, and to the end of the earth." (Acts 1:8)

There could be no mistake that Jesus wanted his church to deliver the gospel of grace "to the end of the earth."

He also wanted his church to "make disciples" of all those who were saved. Being made a disciple means growing to maturity as a child of God. A growing disciple is a person who never stops moving forward on the Grace Pathway.

We can state the mission of the church in two main categories.

The mission of the church is to help people find and follow God.

— THE MISSION OF THE CHURCH IS TO HELP PEOPLE FIND AND FOLLOW GOD.

Most churches have a mission statement. These mission statements may differ slightly, or emphasize different aspects of the mission God has given us. But usually, the two main aspects of our mission can be stated as evangelism and edification.

Evangelism

We help people find God. God loves lost people and wants them found. The church is on a mission to help lost people find their way home to him.

The church consists of saved people.

The world consists of lost people.

God's love for the world, poured into our hearts, compels us to evangelism. The deeper you go into the grace of God, the more passionately you want everyone you know to find the treasure you found when you found Christ.

It is easy for churches to neglect evangelism. But it is our job as Christians and as church leaders to never let that happen.

> ...Yes, woe is me if I do not preach the gospel! (1 Corinthians 9:16b)

Edification

Once people find God in salvation, we help them follow God through edification.

> But we do all things, beloved, for your edification. (2 Corinthians 12:19)

To edify doesn't simply mean to encourage. It's deeper than that. To edify means to build certain structures inside a person's soul. These are structures of thinking and believing, structures of instinct and emotion.

The whole goal is to increasingly reproduce the "mind of Christ" inside the mind of you! This doesn't mean you will lose your personality or anything like that. God's goal is for you to be your truest, deepest self, with all the color added by the beautiful wisdom, courage, and character of Christ.

Edification is simply the process of spiritual growth. It is the Grace Pathway. It is pushing away from the kiddie table, and joining the Feast of Grace with the grown ups. This is the great mission of the church as we go into all the world, bear witness of Christ to the end of the earth, and implement all the grace that is already ours in our glorious mission of multiplying disciples.

THE RITUALS OF THE CHURCH

Jesus instructed the Church to carry on two rituals: baptism and the Lord's Supper.

In churches that are more formal, these rituals are often called *sacraments,* based on the Latin word for "mystery." Under this view, baptism and the Lord's Supper actually convey God's grace to the recipient in a mystical way.

In churches that are less formal, these rituals are usually called *ordinances*, based on the word that means "an orderly practice." Under this view, baptism and the Lord's supper are symbols of the grace that has already been conveyed by faith. They are outward symbols of inner realities. For this reason, many Christians prefer the term *ordinances* over *sacraments.*

Both ordinances symbolize salvation. They do not cause salvation. They do not grant salvation. The ordinances are outward symbols of inner realities, and it is the inner reality that makes all the difference. Are you saved? Then tell the world in the ordinance of baptism, and remind yourself of salvation's cost in the ordinance of communion.

The ordinance of baptism is like a wedding ring. It symbolizes the day a person was saved, and proclaims to the world that this person has made a profession of faith in Jesus Christ. Baptism is usually a one-time event in our lives.

The ordinance of the Lord's Supper, also called Communion or the Eucharist, reminds us of the enormously high cost of our salvation. Jesus said, "Do this in remembrance of me" (1 Corinthians 11:24). The broken bread depicts his body which was broken on Calvary's Cross. The wine depicts his shed blood. The Lord's Supper is a repeated event, because God wants us to never forget the cost and the ground of our salvation.

God is into commemorating because we are into forgetting.

WORSHIP

When the church fulfills her mission of evangelism and edification, God is worshiped.

God's worship is *broader*, because more and more people are worshipping him as the result of evangelism.

God's worship is *deeper*, because we are growing more mature as the result of edification.

In this way, the church fulfills her highest purpose of bringing glory to our great and gracious God.

DIFFERENCES

Sometimes faithful Christians study their Bibles and reach different conclusions. This is natural. If we are doing our best to understand our Bibles, God is always pleased with that.

The biblical teaching on the church is no different.

There are some serious differences on a wide variety of church related topics.

For example, not all Christians agree on how churches should be organized or led. Or on whether we should baptize by dunking, sprinkling, or pouring.

We don't all agree even on when the church officially began. Some say it began with the first believers in the Old Testament, Adam and Eve, whose sins were paid for by the first symbol of the Cross when an animal was sacrificed for them. Others say the church age didn't begin until the New Testament era, and specifically, the outpouring of the Holy Spirit described in Acts 2.

Reasonable Christians might not agree on the relationship between the church and Israel. Or on how to conduct public worship. Or on issues of divorce, the conduct of public worship, and a host of other differences. There is a lively debate over the relationship between the Church and the kingdom of God.

These discussions are important. We should not minimize them. They make us think about our lives in this world and the world to come. They draw us more deeply into the Bible. That's awesome.

At the same time, most church people and church leaders are good at keeping the main thing the main thing. We have a Savior, we have a Bible, we have a mission. In spite of our differences, we who are truly saved are the One Body of Christ.

The main thing is that we help people find and follow God, thus maximizing his worship and glory. If that is happening, and if the Word of God is respected and taught, then let's look past our differences to serve God together in the world. Let's look instead to the wonderful gospel of grace that binds all the people of God together, now and forever.

The church's one foundation is Jesus Christ, her
    Lord;
She is his new creation by water and the Word:
From heav'n he came and sought her to be his holy
    bride;
With his own blood he bought her, and for her life
    he died.

Elect from ev'ry nation, yet one o'er all the earth,
Her charter of salvation: one Lord, one faith, one
    birth;
One holy name she blesses, partakes one holy food,
And to one hope she presses, with ev'ry grace
    endued.

The church shall never perish! Her dear Lord to
    defend,
To guide, sustain, and cherish, is with her to
    the end;
Though there be those that hate her, and false sons
    in her pale,
Against both foe and traitor she ever shall prevail.

'Mid toil and tribulation, and tumult of her war,
She waits the consummation of peace forevermore;
Till with the vision glorious her longing eyes are
    blest,
And the great church victorious shall be the church
    at rest.

Yet she on earth hath union with the God the
    Three in One,
And mystic sweet communion with those whose
    rest is won:
O happy ones and holy! Lord, give us grace
    that we,
Like them, the meek and lowly, on high may dwell
    with thee.

— S. J. STONE, 1866

SANCTIFICATION // GOD'S LIFE IN ME

We believe that God's justifying grace must not be separated from His sanctifying power and purpose. God commands us to love Him supremely and others sacrificially, and to live out our faith with care for one another, compassion toward the poor and justice for the oppressed. With God's Word, the Spirit's power, and fervent prayer in Christ's name, we are to combat the spiritual forces of evil. In obedience to Christ's commission, we are to make disciples among all people, always bearing witness to the gospel in word and deed.

The Grace Pathway is God's plan to lead you through all the stages of spiritual growth. The end result is that the incredible life of Christ would be reflected through you.

To achieve that end result, God brings you through a process called sanctification.

WHAT IS SANCTIFICATION?

Sanctification is the grace-filled work of God in unburying you from the avalanche of sin, and enabling you to live every day with the holiness, joy, and love of Christ flowing through you.

> — SANCTIFICATION IS THE GRACE-FILLED WORK OF GOD IN UNBURYING YOU FROM THE AVALANCHE OF SIN, AND ENABLING YOU TO LIVE EVERY DAY WITH THE HOLINESS, JOY, AND LOVE OF CHRIST FLOWING THROUGH YOU.

Sanctification is God, rewiring the circuits of your mind, instincts, and emotions so they align with his reality and truth.

Sanctification is God strengthening you to be like Christ.

Sanctification is God setting you free from addiction, dysfunction, self-absorption, and every form of bondage.

Sanctification is God lifting you to new levels of holiness in your words, thoughts, and actions.

You could say that to sanctify is to "saint-i-fy." The words *sanctify*, *saint*, and *holy* are different forms of the same word in the biblical languages.

On the day you were saved, God named you a Saint. Saint means *holy one*. This is your true identity in Christ, no matter how you behave. From the moment of salvation onward, you *are* a holy one forever.

Hello, Saint ____ [insert your name here].

But, if a friend followed you around for a week, would

they actually describe you as a holy one? Would they say you were pure and good in all your words, thoughts, and deeds?

Odds are low.

It is super important to understand that no matter how you behave, you are already a saint in God's eyes.[1] He sees the deepest truth about you, and the deepest truth is that there is no flaw in the truest, deepest you.

Just like salvation, there is a past tense, once for all, finality to your position of holiness before God.

However, your everyday practice might not reflect that reality.

This is where sanctification comes in.

In salvation, God calls you a saint—this is a fact about your *life* in Christ.

In sanctification, God begins to make you saintly—this is to become the fact of your *lifestyle* of Christ-in-you (Galatians 2:20).

In salvation, you believe Jesus as Savior.

In sanctification, you increasingly respond to Jesus as Lord.

Justification is *instantaneous*—it happened the nano-second you first believed in Jesus. Sanctification is a *process*—it happens over time as you grow along the Grace Pathway.

Justification is *perfect*—you can't be more justified than you already are in Christ. Sanctification is *imperfect*—there is always more spiritual maturity for us to experience.

Justification is a *birth*. Sanctification is a lifetime of *growth* in grace (2 Peter 2:18,19).

Justification happens at *salvation*. Sanctification follows as your *post-salvation* Christian life journey.

The whole Grace Pathway is a kind of map to a sanctified life.

CONFORMED TO CHRIST

In biblical language, sanctification is you being "conformed to the image" of Christ (Romans 8:29).

The Bible also refers to sanctification as Christ being "formed in you" (Galatians 4:19).

As Christ is formed in you, you are conformed to him. This doesn't mean you will lose your personality. It doesn't mean you will begin speaking in weird, sacred tones. It doesn't mean you will become a weird Christian clone.

When Christ is formed in you and you are conformed to him, it means that you increasingly express Christ's character in your everyday life.

You become more and more holy, like him.

Biblical holiness is not a sterile, joyless compliance with a set of rules.

Biblical holiness is a dynamic journey to wholeness, purpose, and joy. It is the expression of your deepest self, in union with Christ, with all the color added.

Holiness is wholeness.

Wholesomeness.

That is God's gracious plan for you.

Without God's power in sanctification, the imperatives of Christianity are impossible.

Stop sinning. Stop being a jerk. Stop breaking God's laws. Stop messing with people. Stop hurting others.

Be a good person. Love your neighbor. Speak kindly. Give. Serve. Go to those who have never heard, and tell them about your Savior. Rise above your past habits. Rise above your addictions and dysfunctions. Leave those things in the past.

Rise up to your high calling in Christ. Walk worthy of your high calling in Christ.

This is what sanctification is all about.

But it sounds so out of reach.

And it is.

It is humanly impossible.

No one can ever achieve any level of sanctification that pleases God by human strength.

So then, how is sanctification even possible?

THE POWER OF SANCTIFICATION

Many Christians make a big mistake in how they think about their life with God. The mistake is to imagine that *salvation* is by grace and faith, but that *sanctification* is by works.

This is not how God works in your life. God doesn't save you under a grace-system and then sanctify you under a works-system. No. God doesn't change operating systems.

Just as your salvation is powered by grace through faith, so is your sanctification.

The power of sanctification is God himself. When people try to sanctify themselves by their own power, it gets ugly fast.

God says, "I am the Lord who sanctifies you" (Exodus 31:13, Leviticus 20:8).

With human power, a life of holiness is impossible. But with God's power, all things are possible.

If you try to be holy by your own power, you will fail, though you can fake it for a while. If you keep trying, you will eventually become a hypocrite. You will wear a churchy mask, and convince people you've got it all together.

But on the inside, you will feel worn out and messed up.

That's because no one can ever be like Jesus in their own strength.

So in comes God, to give you all the strength you need.

- God empowers sanctification by his Holy Spirit (2 Thessalonians 2:13).
- God empowers sanctification by his Word in you, as you study it (John 17:17).
- God empowers sanctification by Christ in you, as he himself lives through you (Colossians 1:27, John 15:5).
- God empowers sanctification by his love for you, which you reciprocate out of gratitude and joy (Romans 5:5).

The power is God's power, flowing through you.

> ...being confident of this very thing, that He who has begun a good work in you will complete it until the day of Jesus Christ. (Philippians 1:6)

This is the "good work" that matters most in our lives. It is God's good work of salvation and sanctification. God began your salvation by his power and grace. God will mature you in sanctification by his power and grace too.

When does God's power flow through you? As often as you operate in faith (1 Corinthians 2:5).[2]

> I have been crucified with Christ; it is no longer I who live, but Christ lives in me; and the life which I now live in the flesh I live by faith in the Son of God, who loved me and gave Himself for me. (Galatians 2:20)

Sanctification means that all the imperatives of God's

Word are powered by God's grace, as Christ himself lives in us and through us by faith.

> — SANCTIFICATION MEANS THAT ALL THE IMPERATIVES OF GOD'S WORD ARE POWERED BY GOD'S GRACE.

THE PURPOSE OF SANCTIFICATION

The first purpose of sanctification is love.

Love is the ultimate fulfillment of the plan of God. Love for God. Love for your family. Love for the people around you. Love for the world for whom Christ died.

> Now the purpose of the commandment is love from a pure heart, from a good conscience, and from sincere faith, (1 Timothy 1:5)

This will be God's own love, flowing through you, as water flows through a channel. As Christians, we are to be known by our self-giving love. The beautiful thing is that, as we grow along the Grace Pathway, we are so filled and made whole by God's grace, we can begin to give of ourselves without losing ourselves.

With this love, we will care for one another, for society, for people who have been treated unjustly, and for those whose lives are extra difficult.

Sanctification enables you "to do justly, / To love mercy, / And to walk humbly with your God" (Micah 6:8).

Another purpose of sanctification is spiritual warfare.

This means that we engage our lives in fighting the devil's lies—the unreal worldview that infects our culture today.

Sanctification is how God equips spiritual champions for the struggles of everyday life.

Sanctification is how we live in victory over every dark force that would hold us down.

Yet another purpose of sanctification is a natural desire and effort to help lost people be saved.

One sign of maturity in grace is the desire for everybody you know to find the treasure you found when you found Christ.

Sanctification makes you a joyful and magnetic witness to the power of Jesus in the world.

LIKE AN ICEBERG

While we believe that "God's justifying grace must not be separated from his sanctifying power and purpose," we also believe that justification and sanctification must not be confused. One is the root, and one is the fruit.

Sometimes a person is saved, and their sanctification seems like it's taking forever. Some Christians become very judgmental of others at this point. They might even question whether or not the person was actually saved.

That's not our place.

Besides, it shows a misunderstanding of sanctification.

Think of an iceberg. The vast majority of it is underwater. You can't see it.

So it is with sanctification. The majority of sanctification is invisible because it is internal. God is healing the broken places inside a person's heart. God is renewing their mind. God is turning around their thinking. He is birthing "repentance" within them, so that they might "change their mind" about themselves, their powers, their past, and their future. He is renewing them in the "inner person" (Ephesians 3:16).

God does all this by stitching Scripture to a person's inmost being.

Just because you can't see their "life change" doesn't mean God isn't working. Be patient. Don't judge. God looks at the heart, and that is where his most important work takes place.

All the life-affirming, love-creating imperatives of the Christian life become possible as you grow in sanctifying grace and respond to the great love that has been poured out on you in Christ.

Take my life and let it be
consecrated, Lord, to thee.
Take my moments and my days;
let them flow in endless praise,
let them flow in endless praise.

Take my hands and let them move
at the impulse of thy love.
Take my feet and let them be
swift and beautiful for thee,
swift and beautiful for thee.

Take my voice and let me sing
always, only, for my King.
Take my lips and let them be
filled with messages from thee,
filled with messages from thee.

Take my silver and my gold;
not a mite would I withhold.
Take my intellect and use

every power as thou shalt choose,
every power as thou shalt choose.

Take my will and make it thine;
it shall be no longer mine.
Take my heart it is thine own;
it shall be thy royal throne,
it shall be thy royal throne.

Take my love; my Lord, I pour
at thy feet its treasure store.
Take myself, and I will be
ever, only, all for thee,
ever, only, all for thee.

— FRANCES RIDLEY
HAVERGAL, 1874

---

1. We talked about this back in Grace Pathway Milestone 2.2, *You're Richer Than You Think.*
2. We'll go deeper in Milestone 4.1, *Living and Sharing Your Faith.*

SATAN AND DEMONS // GOD'S NEMESIS

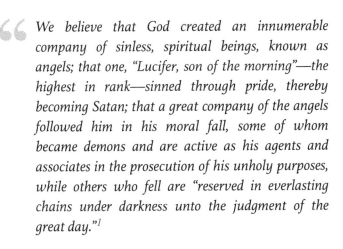

> We believe that God created an innumerable company of sinless, spiritual beings, known as angels; that one, "Lucifer, son of the morning"—the highest in rank—sinned through pride, thereby becoming Satan; that a great company of the angels followed him in his moral fall, some of whom became demons and are active as his agents and associates in the prosecution of his unholy purposes, while others who fell are "reserved in everlasting chains under darkness unto the judgment of the great day."[1]
>
> — DALLAS THEOLOGICAL SEMINARY

There is more to this world than we can see with our eyes, view through telescopes, or explain through science and math.

We are living in a profoundly spiritual universe—something most of the world takes for granted, but the Western world has often forgotten.

It is as if a veil separates the material realm we can access through our five senses from a spiritual realm we can only discover through Scripture. Unless God reveals these things to us, we have no way of knowing about them.

> While we do not look at the things which are seen, but at the things which are not seen. For the things which are seen are temporary, but the things which are not seen are eternal. (2 Corinthians 4:18)

The spiritual realm is alive with realities to stagger the imagination. God and the devil, angels and demons, heaven and hell, truth and deception—these things are as real as the ground on which we walk.

There is a great deal of superstition around the spiritual realm. Folklore, visions, prophetic utterances, seers, and seances must never be used to learn about this realm. These sources are deceptive. They create confusion and fear. God's Word is all we need, and God's Word is all we should seek.

The spiritual realm is greater than the material realm. The eternal truths of heaven undergird everything in our temporal experience. It is God who makes all things real. From God's nature and character flow the laws that govern everything in space and time—everything science, philosophy, and math might ever discover comes from him.

> And [Jesus Christ] is before all things, and in Him all things consist. (Colossians 1:17)

One of the more startling revelations of Scripture is the existence of angels and demons. These are powerful spiritual beings, possessing intelligence and will.

God's Word tells us the struggles of our everyday lives involves them.

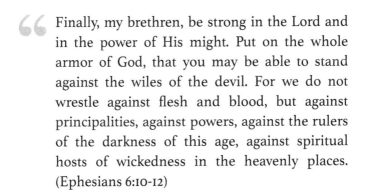

> Finally, my brethren, be strong in the Lord and in the power of His might. Put on the whole armor of God, that you may be able to stand against the wiles of the devil. For we do not wrestle against flesh and blood, but against principalities, against powers, against the rulers of the darkness of this age, against spiritual hosts of wickedness in the heavenly places. (Ephesians 6:10-12)

The principalities and powers refer to fallen spiritual beings. Let's think through who these beings are and how this matters for our lives today.

ANGELS

God created angels. As we learned in *Knowing God* (Grace Pathway 3.1), God is omnipotent—infinite in power. Neither angels, nor demons, nor the devil are omnipotent. Their power doesn't come close to God's. Nor are they omniscient like He is.

Angels are spiritual beings, meaning they do not occupy bodies made of matter, like ours. Because they are spiritual, they are normally invisible to us. However, the Bible records many times when they appeared to people in visible, and sometimes human, form.[2]

Though they are not omnipotent, they are still very powerful. Peter says "they are greater in power and might" than humans (2 Peter 2:11). It only took one angel to destroy an army of 185,000 Assyrians, only one angel to effect the judgment of God on Egypt, and only one angel to shut the mouths of hungry lions in Daniel's day (Isaiah 37:36, Numbers 20:16, Daniel 6:22).

The Bible outlines various ranks of angels, but does not go into detail. It is important that where the Bible is clear, we dig in and study. But where the Bible is silent, we are wise enough not to speculate. And we should certainly never turn to other sources to fill in the gaps the Bible intentionally leaves unfilled.

To describe the ranks of angels (fallen and unfallen), the Bible uses terms like archangels, authorities, powers, principalities, rulers, cherubim, and seraphim. Other than studying the Greek and Hebrew terms underlying these words, we have very little detail in Scripture as to how these different ranks operate.

The word for angels simply means messengers. Angels are God's messengers and God's servants. There are angels flying around the throne of God, perpetually praising his infinite holiness (Isaiah 6:3).

Angels and humans are very different kinds of beings. Humans do not become angels when they die, no matter how good they may have been. Humans remain humans, and angels remain angels (fallen or unfallen), forever.

LUCIFER BECAME SATAN

After God created the angels, he set one angel over them all. That angel was called Lucifer, which means shining light. The Bible describes this mighty angel's beauty in striking metaphor:

 You were in Eden, the garden of God; Every precious stone was your covering: The sardius, topaz, and diamond, Beryl, onyx, and jasper, Sapphire, turquoise, and emerald with gold. The workmanship of your timbrels and pipes Was prepared for you on the day you were created. "You were the anointed cherub who covers; I established you; You were on the holy mountain of God; You walked back and forth in the midst of fiery stones. You were perfect in your ways from the day you were created, Till iniquity was found in you. (Ezekiel 28:13-15)

The iniquity that was found in Lucifer was pride.

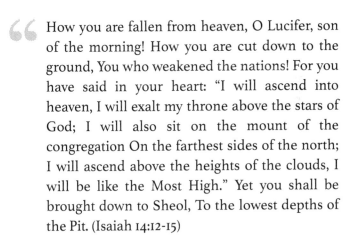

How you are fallen from heaven, O Lucifer, son of the morning! How you are cut down to the ground, You who weakened the nations! For you have said in your heart: "I will ascend into heaven, I will exalt my throne above the stars of God; I will also sit on the mount of the congregation On the farthest sides of the north; I will ascend above the heights of the clouds, I will be like the Most High." Yet you shall be brought down to Sheol, To the lowest depths of the Pit. (Isaiah 14:12-15)

With astonishing arrogance, Lucifer deluded himself into thinking he could be "like the Most High," making himself equal with God.

This is not only supreme hubris, it is also supreme foolishness and immeasurable irrationality.

Lucifer, the Bright One, became Satan, the Adversary. Jesus said, "I saw Satan fall like lightning from heaven" (Luke 10:18).

When Satan fell, it is likely he drew about a third of the angels with him. These fallen angels we now call demons.

> 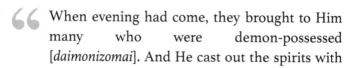 And another sign appeared in heaven: behold, a great, fiery red dragon having seven heads and ten horns, and seven diadems on his heads. His tail drew a third of the stars of heaven and threw them to the earth. And the dragon stood before the woman who was ready to give birth, to devour her Child as soon as it was born. (Revelation 12:3, 4)

Lucifer's name was changed. He is now called Satan or the devil—words that mean Adversary. The angels that fell with him are now called demons. The angels who never fell are simply called angels, holy angels, or the elect angels.

Humans do not become angels or demons when they die. We do not turn into ghosts or anything like that. When we die, we remain our eternal selves, either with or without God (more on this in chapter 13).

DEMONS AND POSSESSION

The term "demon possession" is not exactly found in the Bible, though many translations use the term. The biblical word, *daimonizomai*, is a verb. It means something like to be harassed, attacked, or harmed by demons. It could be translated *demonized*. This is a different meaning than possession, which implies ownership.

> When evening had come, they brought to Him many who were demon-possessed [*daimonizomai*]. And He cast out the spirits with

a word, and healed all who were sick...
(Matthew 8:16)

The people of the city brought to Jesus many who were *demonized*. As we study God's Word, we realize that this means to be influenced by the lies and deceptions of the devil to varying degrees.

These degrees range from confusion and sadness on one end to an outright embrace of evil and destruction on the other. In extreme cases, a person's personality can be so overwhelmed by evil that they manifest what is commonly thought of as demon possession.

No Christian can be possessed or indwelled by a demon, as we are owned and indwelled by God. You are sealed by God's Spirit, guarded by God's power, and bought by God himself. Your *ideas* can be messed up by the dark side, but your *being* cannot be possessed or invaded by demons.

> He has delivered us from the power of darkness and conveyed us into the kingdom of the Son of His love. (Colossians 1:13).

Again, the devil's power works across a range of intensity. However this range of intensity works, the primary way the devil influences people today is simple. *The devil works overtime to get us to believe his lies.*

Lies about God.

Lies about who we are.

Lies about our world.

Lies about what will make us happy or about why we are sad.

Lies about our past, our present, and our future.

Lies about the other people in our lives.

The devil works through philosophies, through world views, through a world-system. The prevailing philosophies of our culture are under the devil's sway (1 John 5:19). But they don't always seem that way.

That's because the devil makes his lies as appealing and beautiful as he possibly can. He will do anything to seduce people to the dark side, presenting himself masquerading as an "angel of light" (2 Corinthians 11:14).

The Bible teaches us about a spiritual warfare. This battle is being waged every single day all around us. It is something for believers to be aware of, but not afraid of. God himself protects us, and he has provided us invincible weapons for the fight (Ephesians 6:10-17).

The primary weapon is building God's truth into the core of your existence, and developing a strong bond of love with God.

That is why God's people must routinely engage with the Bible. As we bring our thoughts into alignment with God's truth, we are delivered from the demonic lies that infect our culture and diminish our lives.

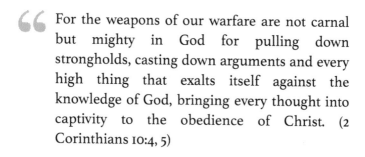 For the weapons of our warfare are not carnal but mighty in God for pulling down strongholds, casting down arguments and every high thing that exalts itself against the knowledge of God, bringing every thought into captivity to the obedience of Christ. (2 Corinthians 10:4, 5)

VICTORY IS CERTAIN

There are two opposite extremes Christians should avoid when it comes to Satan and demons.

One extreme is skepticism—to deny or doubt their existence and influence in our lives and our world.

The other extreme is obsession—to wring our hands over them and to blame them for everything wrong in our lives and our world.

Yes, the devil and demons are real. But so is God, and his reality is infinitely greater and more impactful. God, through Jesus Christ, has already won the victory. The Holy Spirit of God is mightier than the strongest demons, and infinitely stronger than the devil himself.

> You are of God, little children, and have overcome them, because He who is in you is greater than he who is in the world. (1 John 4:4)

The wonderful truth is that Christ has already overcome the dark side. He did this through his Cross, Resurrection, and Ascension.

His victory is complete.

Because his victory is complete, ours is too.

You don't have to win the victory over Satan—Jesus has already done that for you and on your behalf. Your job is to believe the victory is won, take your stand in God's truth, and live every day in victory, truth, and grace. "Therefore submit to God. Resist the devil and he will flee from you" (James 4:7).

One day, we will see the "complete completion" of God's victory with our own eyes. On that day, God will cast Satan and his demons into the Lake of Fire that has been prepared for them (Matthew 25:46).

The important thing to remember is this: the devil and demons have no power in our lives than what we give them. The main way we empower their evil is through believing their lies and embracing sinful thoughts and actions.

But, when we embrace God's Grace Pathway, and believe God's Word, we pull up the roots of any influence the dark side has in our lives.

You can live in peace.

You can live in victory.

This is your great privilege as a joint-heir of the victorious King of kings and Lord of lords.

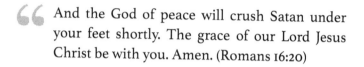

> And the God of peace will crush Satan under your feet shortly. The grace of our Lord Jesus Christ be with you. Amen. (Romans 16:20)

---

*A mighty fortress is our God, a bulwark never
    failing;*
*Our helper he, amid the flood of mortal ills
    prevailing.*
For still our ancient foe does seek to work us woe;
*His craft and power are great, and armed with
    cruel hate,*
On earth is not his equal.

*Did we in our own strength confide, our striving
    would be losing,*
*Were not the right Man on our side, the Man of
    God's own choosing.*
You ask who that may be? Christ Jesus, it is he;
Lord Sabaoth his name, from age to age the same;
And he must win the battle.

*And though this world, with devils filled, should
    threaten to undo us,*

We will not fear, for God has willed his truth to
triumph through us.
The prince of darkness grim, we tremble not
for him;
His rage we can endure, for lo! his doom is sure;
One little word shall fell him.

That Word above all earthly powers no thanks to
them abideth;
The Spirit and the gifts are ours through him who
with us sideth.
Let goods and kindred go, this mortal life also;
The body they may kill: God's truth abideth still;
His kingdom is forever!

— MARTIN LUTHER, 1529

---

1. From the Full Doctrinal Statement of Dallas Theological Seminary. The statement adds the following Scripture references: (Isa. 14:12–17; Ezek. 28:11–19; 1 Tim. 3:6; 2 Pet. 2:4; Jude 6). From https://www.dts.edu/about/doctrinal-statement/ retrieved August 23, 2019.
2. Gen.19; Judges 2:1; 6:11-22; Matt.1:20; Luke 1:26; John 20:12.

THE SECOND COMING // GOD'S VICTORY

> *We believe in the personal, bodily and premillennial[1] return of our Lord Jesus Christ. The coming of Christ, at a time known only to God, demands constant expectancy and, as our blessed hope, motivates the believer to godly living, sacrificial service and energetic mission.*

Jesus promised his followers "I will come again" (John 14:3). When he ascended to heaven, two angels said, "This same Jesus, who was taken up from you into heaven, will so come in like manner as you saw Him go into heaven" (Acts 1:11).

Jesus is coming again.

We still await the fulfillment of that promise.

The Second Coming of Christ gives shape and definition to all of world history.

We can think of Christ's return as a series of related events. Each event fulfills numerous prophecies of Scripture. Each event fulfills the long-developing purposes of God, and finalizes all the wonderful promises of God.

Like many important doctrines, reasonable, Bible-believing Christians disagree on certain details. While all believe that Jesus will come again, not all agree on the sequence or timing of end-time events.

The reason for these disagreements can be found in the nature of biblical prophecy. Much of end-times prophecy overflows with imagery and metaphor. For example:

> Immediately I was in the Spirit; and behold, a throne set in heaven, and One sat on the throne. And He who sat there was like a jasper and a sardius stone in appearance; and there was a rainbow around the throne, in appearance like an emerald. Around the throne were twenty-four thrones, and on the thrones I saw twenty-four elders sitting, clothed in white robes; and they had crowns of gold on their heads. And from the throne proceeded lightnings, thunderings, and voices. Seven lamps of fire were burning before the throne, which are the seven Spirits of God. (Revelation 4:2-5)

Old Testament prophecies can be equally loaded with imagery:

> The ten horns are ten kings Who shall arise from this kingdom. And another shall rise after them; He shall be different from the first ones, And shall subdue three kings. He shall speak pompous words against the Most High, Shall persecute the saints of the Most High, And shall intend to change times and law. Then the saints

shall be given into his hand For a time and times and half a time. (Daniel 7:24, 25)

I am by no means suggesting that these texts are impossible to correctly interpret. I am suggesting that they are tougher than most, and that reasonable, faithful Bible scholars can disagree, even after they have done the hard work of biblical interpretation.

As long as we agree that Jesus is coming again, we might not agree on the details, and we might not agree on the exact sequence. But we can still love each other. We can still work together on the all-important mission of helping people find and follow God.

Here are some of the main events related to the second coming of Christ. As we go through them, we will mention where Christians might have differing interpretations.

THE RAPTURE

There is a lot of discussion around the Rapture. There is significant debate on whether or not there even is a Rapture.

The Rapture is the event in which Jesus Christ returns, not to earth, but to the sky, to gather up believers from the earth, and to escort them back to heaven.

 For the Lord Himself will descend from heaven with a shout, with the voice of an archangel, and with the trumpet of God. And the dead in Christ will rise first. Then we who are alive and remain shall be *caught up* together with them in the clouds to meet the Lord in the air. And thus we shall always be with the Lord. (1 Thessalonians 4:16, 17, emphasis added)

In the Rapture, Jesus returns to "the clouds." He brings along believers who have previously died—their souls/spirits accompany him.

Christians who are still on earth will rise up to the clouds to meet Jesus. In that same moment, their bodies will be instantly transformed with new glories and powers fit for heaven. This is often called the Resurrection Body, because it will be like the body Jesus had after his resurrection.

At the same time, the bodies of Christians who have already died will be miraculously reconstituted. These bodies will be transformed into Resurrection bodies, then resurrected, and finally reunited with their original owners (1 Corinthians 15:51, 52).

Though the word Rapture is not in our English Bibles, a form of the word appears in the Latin translations of the Bible. The words *caught up* appear in Latin as *rapiemur,* which gives us the English word *Rapture*. It means to catch away, to suddenly snatch.

The Rapture will happen so fast, it will seem as if Christians on earth just disappeared. The Bible says it will happen "in a moment, in the twinkling of an eye" (1 Corinthians 15:52).

One area where Christians might not agree is on whether or not the Rapture in the clouds is a separate event from the Second Coming to earth. If it is a separate event, then it is *part one* of the Second Coming, and *part two*—in which Jesus returns to earth—won't happen till seven years later. If the Rapture is not a separate event, then all these things will happen all at once when the Lord returns.

Another topic up for debate is whether the Rapture happens before, after, or during the middle of the event called the Tribulation (which we will outline in the next section). These views are called pre-trib, post-trib, and mid-trib Rapture views.

The important thing is that God's Word is overwhelmingly clear that Jesus Christ is personally coming again.

THE TRIBULATION

The Tribulation is a period of unprecedented destruction and death on earth. Scripture indicates it will last for seven years.

- "For then there will be great tribulation, such as has not been since the beginning of the world until this time, no, nor ever shall be. (Matthew 24:21)
- Then he shall confirm a covenant with many for one week; But in the middle of the week He shall bring an end to sacrifice and offering. And on the wing of abominations shall be one who makes desolate, Even until the consummation, which is determined, Is poured out on the desolate." (Daniel 9:27)

Many interpreters suggest the "seven weeks" in Daniel is a reference to a seven year tribulation.

THE ANTICHRIST

We can look at the Tribulation as Satan throwing a global temper tantrum in his never-ceasing attempts to usurp the place of Jesus Christ. He will focus his attempts through the rise of a world leader the Bible calls the Antichrist.

The Antichrist is a human person, energized by Satan, who

will attempt to replace Christ and bring in a false kingdom of God through deception and force.

> Little children, it is the last hour; and as you have heard that the Antichrist is coming, even now many antichrists have come, by which we know that it is the last hour. (1 John 2:18)

It is likely the Antichrist will emerge on the global stage promising peace, prosperity, and progress, but delivering war, violence, and chaos. Only Jesus Christ can rule this unruly world (2 Corinthians 11:14).

The Bible calls the Antichrist the Beast (Revelation 13:13) and the Man of Lawlessness (1 Thessalonians 2:3). He is empowered by Satan, "the dragon," himself (Revelation 13:2).

The Antichrist requires the mysterious Mark of the Beast, some kind of bodily mark or implant required to "buy or sell" anything. It is in some undefined way connected with the number 666.

> He causes all, both small and great, rich and poor, free and slave, to receive a mark on their right hand or on their foreheads, and that no one may buy or sell except one who has the mark or the name of the beast, or the number of his name. Here is wisdom. Let him who has understanding calculate the number of the beast, for it is the number of a man: His number is six hundred and sixty-six. (Revelation 13:16-18)

The Mark of the Beast is also a mark of allegiance to Satan, and those who receive it will seal their fate (Revelation 19:20).

Christians have identified different rulers over the centuries as the Antichrist, ranging from Nero to popes to whoever is the latest president. All have proven to be wrong.

We have also proposed countless theories over the Mark of the Beast. All of these have been wrong too.

It's best not to speculate.

The Antichrist is assisted by the False Prophet, the leader of a false world-religion (Revelation 13:15). The False Prophet demands the worship of the Antichrist.

The political, moral, and military conflict brought on by the Antichrist in the Tribulation period boils over, bringing on the mother of all wars.

ARMAGEDDON

> For they are spirits of demons, performing signs, which go out to the kings of the earth and of the whole world, to gather them to the battle of that great day of God Almighty. . . . And they gathered them together to the place called in Hebrew, Armageddon. (Revelation 16:14, 16)

The greatest world war earth has ever known will break out, the Battle of Armageddon. It will be history's worst bloodbath (Revelation 14:20).

The Battle of Armageddon is earth's last attempt to throw off the reign of Jesus Christ, using military power to destroy Israel once for all, and to install the reign of the devil and his surrogates.

Named after a hill overlooking the vast plain of Megiddo, the armies of earth will converge in Israel. The floodgates of violence and demonic infiltration will be opened, and blood will flow freely (Revelation 14:20).

THE SECOND COMING

At the height of the Battle of Armageddon, Jesus Christ will return. He will ride out of heaven with armies of saints and angels.

 "Then the sign of the Son of Man will appear in heaven, and then all the tribes of the earth will mourn, and they will see the Son of Man coming on the clouds of heaven with power and great glory. "And He will send His angels with a great sound of a trumpet, and they will gather together His elect from the four winds, from one end of heaven to the other." (Matthew 24:30, 31)

The Second Coming of Christ is his dramatic return to earth to defeat his enemies, usher in his kingdom, punish evil, and fulfill all his promises to Israel, the world, and the church.

Christ's return will be glorious and swift. He will destroy the armies arrayed against Israel (Revelation 19:15). He will devastate the Antichrist and the False Prophet (2 Thessalonians 2:8). He will imprison Satan in the Abyss to await his final doom (Revelation 20:1-3).

We who know Jesus will return alongside him. He will be the triumphant, all-conquering Hero. We will be soldiers in his victorious army. What a day that will be!

THE MILLENNIUM

God promised the world a king, and this is the day he keeps his promise.

God promised to Christ a kingdom, and this is the day God keeps that promise too.

When Jesus takes his rightful throne, with the thunderous applause of the redeemed cosmos and the holy angels —in that glorious moment the curse of sin is lifted, the fall is reversed, death is crippled, and the love of God, the peace of God, and the joy of God take hold of all our hearts in ways we can't begin to imagine.

What a day that will be!

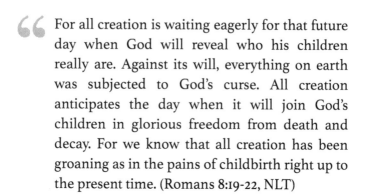

> For all creation is waiting eagerly for that future day when God will reveal who his children really are. Against its will, everything on earth was subjected to God's curse. All creation anticipates the day when it will join God's children in glorious freedom from death and decay. For we know that all creation has been groaning as in the pains of childbirth right up to the present time. (Romans 8:19-22, NLT)

Only Jesus can create heaven on earth. The Church can't. The government can't. The world's philosophers, and rich people, and wise people, and bright people, and elite people can't. The devil can't.

Only Jesus.

When Jesus returns to set up his millennial kingdom:

- He chains Satan and throws him into the bottomless pit. (Rev. 20:1-3)
- He restores Israel, so that the Jewish race realizes he is their Messiah and King. (Rev. 7:1-7, Dan. 12:5-7; Ezek. 20:33-38).
- He sweeps away the governments of the earth.

- He sets up his righteous government over all the earth.

Christians may differ on the nature of this kingdom. There are three main views on the millennium.

- *Premillennialism* — Jesus returns to earth *before* the millennium to set up his earthly kingdom.
- *Postmillennialism*— Jesus returns to earth *after* the millennium, which is a golden age on earth established without the personal presence of Jesus, but by his power and grace. Postmillennialism makes it the church's primary mission to create heaven on earth through doing social good. Then, only *after* the kingdom has been established by us, the King returns.
- *Amillennialism*—Jesus returns to earth, and immediately ushers in the Eternal State (described in the next section) without any rule or reign on earth. This position basically skips the millennium, and interprets Scriptures about the millennium in a non-literal way.

The issues in this debate are complex and beyond the scope of this book.

However, many evangelicals have tended toward premillennialism for very good reasons. If there is going to be such a thing as the kingdom of God on earth, it is impossible to see how this could be accomplished in a post-millennial system.

Furthermore, without King Jesus at the helm of an earthly kingdom, it's hard to see how God has kept his promises to Israel of a Promised Land, and to David of a worldwide throne, under the amillennial system.

Finally, taking biblical prophecies at face value, especially those of Revelation 20:2-7, would favor a premillennial return of Christ, along with a literal millennium on earth.

JUDGMENT DAY

To believe in the justice of God is to believe in a coming day of judgment. The two cannot be separated.

While Scripture describes a variety of judgment days, there are two main ones: there is a coming judgment day for believers in Jesus, and there is a separate coming judgment day for unbelievers.

- *For believers:* The Judgment Seat of Christ. (2 Corinthians 5:10)
- *For unbelievers:* The Great White Throne Judgment. (Revelation 20:11-15)

Let's consider these one at a time.

The Judgment Seat of Christ is the day God evaluates the works of his own children, who are already saved and bound for heaven, to determine their rewards in heaven.

ONLY BELIEVERS WILL APPEAR at this judgment. In this case, the word judgment is not about final justice. This is because final justice for believers in Jesus was finalized at the Cross. The day Jesus died on the Cross is the day of judgment for all your sins.

However, in this Judgment Day, your sins are not even

mentioned. There is no condemnation for you, and because of Calvary, no chance of it (Romans 8:1, Psalm 103:10-12).

The Judgment Seat of Christ is Evaluation Day for you. It will be God's way of pouring out on you wonderful rewards for every moment of faith in your life. Every speck of grace you have embraced in this life will be multiplied in heaven to provide overwhelming capacity to enjoy everlasting blessings beyond comprehension. Every inch of forward progress you have made along the Grace Pathway will be noticed, multiplied, and amply rewarded. So keep going!

The Judgment Seat of Christ is called the Bema Seat in Greek (2 Corinthians 5:10), as this is where officials would hand out awards in the ancient Olympics. It is described in 1 Corinthians 3:10-13.

After the Judgment Seat of Christ, we will immediately enter Heaven, and run into the outstretched arms of our precious Savior who has brought all this grace into our lives.

THE GREAT WHITE Throne Judgment is the day when all unbelievers stand before God for final judgment, and receive the condemnation their sins so richly deserve.

This judgment is the one most people think of when they hear the terms Judgment Day. Only unbelievers, of all ages of human history, will appear at the Great White Throne Judgment. It is an awesome and awful display of the righteous wrath of a just and holy God.

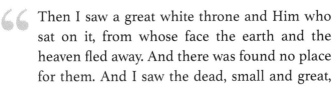

Then I saw a great white throne and Him who sat on it, from whose face the earth and the heaven fled away. And there was found no place for them. And I saw the dead, small and great, standing before God, and books were opened. And another book was opened, which is the Book of Life. And the dead were judged according to their works, by the things which were written in the books. The sea gave up the dead who were in it, and Death and Hades delivered up the dead who were in them. And they were judged, each one according to his works. Then Death and Hades were cast into the lake of fire. This is the second death. And anyone not found written in the Book of Life was cast into the lake of fire. (Revelation 20:11-15)

God judges sin. One look at Calvary proves it. People will either accept God's judgment for their sin, or they will stand before a righteous Judge to pay for their own sins.

The prophets warned, "Prepare to meet your God" (Amos 4:12). The apostles warned, "It is a fearful thing to fall into the hands of the Living God" (Hebrews 10:31). Jesus said, "Fear Him who is able to destroy both soul and body in hell" (Matthew 10:28).

The reality of Judgment Day should fill us with compassion for lost people, and a desire to help them find Christ.

We will talk more about heaven and hell in the next chapter.

WHEN ADAM AND EVE SINNED, the world, everybody and everything fell under a curse. Every bit of creation is in pain. Our lives prove it. This is why life is hard. This is why pain happens.

This fallen world is a morally broken pain machine.

But on that glorious day, when Jesus is revealed in all his splendor, when Jesus takes his rightful throne with a shout and a trumpet blast and the thunderous applause of the redeemed cosmos and the holy angels... in that glorious day the curse is lifted, the fall is reversed, death is crippled, and the love of God, the peace of God, and the joy of God take hold of all our hearts in ways we can't begin to imagine.

What a day that will be!

Lift up your heads, pilgrims a-weary,
See day's approach now crimson the sky;
Night shadows flee, and your Beloved,
Awaited with longing, at last draweth nigh.

He is coming again, He is coming again,
The very same Jesus, rejected of men;
He is coming again, He is coming again,
With pow'r and great glory, He is coming again!

Dark was the night, sin warred against us;
Heavy the load of sorrow we bore;
But now we see signs of His coming;
Our hearts glow within us, joy's cup runneth o'er!

O blessed hope! O blissful promise!
Filling our hearts with rapture divine;

O day of days! Hail Thy appearing!
Thy transcendent glory forever shall shine!

Even so come, precious Lord Jesus;
Creation awaits redemption to see;
Caught up in clouds, soon we shall meet Thee;
O blessed assurance, forever with Thee!

— MABEL J. CAMP, 1913

---

1. Shortly before this book went to press, the Evangelical Free Church of America changed their position on a premillennial return of Christ. Their statement removed the word *premillennial* and substituted the word *glorious*. It is easy enough to find their complete rationale online, though the main one is to appeal to a broader swath of evangelical leaders. The Grace Pathway advocates a premillennial position, and does so with love and respect for other positions.

HEAVEN AND HELL // GOD'S GLORY

" *We believe that God commands everyone everywhere to believe the gospel by turning to Him in repentance and receiving the Lord Jesus Christ. We believe that God will raise the dead bodily and judge the world, assigning the unbeliever to condemnation and eternal conscious punishment and the believer to eternal blessedness and joy with the Lord in the new heaven and the new earth, to the praise of His glorious grace. Amen.*

E very author looks forward to that glorious moment when they can finally type the words, The End. In the grand story we find in the Bible, when we get to The End, we discover it is nothing but a new beginning.

The doctrinal name for this new beginning is the Eternal State. In the Eternal State, God finalizes his purposes for the original creation. The cosmos as we know it comes to an end, and God creates a New Heaven and New Earth.

- For behold, I create new heavens and a new earth;

And the former shall not be remembered or come
to mind. (Isaiah 65:17)
- Nevertheless we, according to His promise, look
for new heavens and a new earth in which
righteousness dwells. (2 Peter 3:13)
- Now I saw a new heaven and a new earth, for the
first heaven and the first earth had passed away.
Also there was no more sea. (Revelation 21:1)

In the Eternal State, every person, angel, demon, and
molecule will exist forever in a correct relationship to God.
This means some will be in heaven and others will be in the
Lake of Fire, commonly called Hell.

THE LAKE OF FIRE (HELL)

In all of Scripture, it is Jesus who spoke the most about hell.

- And these will go away into everlasting
punishment, but the righteous into eternal life.
(Matthew 25:46)
- Serpents, brood of vipers! How can you escape the
condemnation of hell. (Matthew 23:33)

Biblical teaching on hell is woven throughout God's
Word. It is painful to think about, and a source of friction
between Christians and the world.

God's justice is the ultimate reason for hell. If God were
not just, there would be no hell. Evil would create no imbalance in the universe that needed divine correction. Everyone
from axe-murderers to genocidal Hitlers to child abusers
would get off totally free. Evil would win in the end.

Consider the alternative to hell: *do you really want to live in a universe where evil goes unpunished?* Imagine a universe where the Supreme Being accepts evil or tolerates it. Imagine a universe where God is indifferent to evil, cruelty, or abuse. Do you really want that kind of God or that kind of universe?

We instinctively know that love can't win if holiness loses.

If you were constructing a universe, and really thinking about it, you would construct a universe in which God was holy, and the evil-doers of the cosmos got punished. Any other universe would be intolerable. That is exactly why the Bible makes so much sense. It echoes our heart's deepest instincts.

May I suggest that is because our heart's instincts and the Bible's words share the same Author.

Hell means that evil has a far-away parking place, and God is fair forever. The bad guys get away with nothing. The force that hurt you, the person who exploited you, and the powers that consumed you, get their due. Hell proves that God takes it personally when people hurt people (sin); he doesn't just yawn and turn the other way.

If you're evil's *victim* (and you are), you might take comfort in that.

If you're evil's *perpetrator* (and you are), you might find terror in that.

Welcome to the biblical worldview.

Many people ask how a loving God could ever send anybody to hell.

The more difficult question is to ask how a holy God could welcome sinners into heaven.

 — THE MORE DIFFICULT QUESTION IS
TO ASK HOW A HOLY GOD COULD
WELCOME SINNERS INTO HEAVEN.

Scripture is clear that hell is eternal. Jesus uses the exact same word to describe the duration of both eternal life and eternal punishment (Matthew 25:46). This means that God does not shut off a soul, like a light switch. This also means that people do not get a second chance after they die.

The decision to receive or not receive Jesus in this life determines a person's destiny forever. The Bible says, "And as it is appointed for men to die once, but after this the judgment" (Hebrews 9:27).

Hell proves that God takes human freedom with infinite seriousness. God will not cram salvation down anybody's throat. You are free to believe, and free not to believe, in Jesus. John Hannah said, "No one who is ever in hell will be able to say to God, 'You put me here,' and no one who is in heaven will ever be able to say, 'I put myself here.'"

While those in hell will be in pain, they will also remain defiant and angry against God. This is the meaning of the phrase "gnashing of teeth" in places like Matthew 8:12:[1] "But the sons of the kingdom will be cast out into outer darkness. There will be weeping and gnashing of teeth."

Some have said that hell is the best God can do for a person who refuses the sacrifice of Jesus. Others have suggested the gates of hell are locked from the inside.

Any person with an ounce of compassion who thinks about hell will be gripped with an urgent desire to help lost people find the Savior.

As horrible as the Eternal State will be for those who have never turned to God in faith (by changing their minds about Jesus in repentance), the delights of heaven will be exponentially more wonderful.

HEAVEN

All doctrine, all theology, all history, and all God's promises point here. When all is said and done, you will open your eyes in glory.

> And God will wipe away every tear from their eyes; there shall be no more death, nor sorrow, nor crying. There shall be no more pain, for the former things have passed away." (Revelation 21:4)

I don't know what it's going to feel like, smell like, sound like, look like, or taste like. I don't think human language can describe it or human minds can grasp it. It's a feast. It's a party. It's an adventure. It's a mission. It's infinitely better than you can ask or dream.

God has written a story. It arcs from his pre-creation solitude to the acclamation of ten thousand times ten thousand ransomed beings in the new heavens and new earth. Each of us lives, dies, and lives again as interconnected subplots in God's grand story. From our perspective on this anthill called earth, the story unfolds one nerve-wracking line at a time. But from God's perspective on Mount Eternity, the story has already been written to a breathtakingly satisfying conclusion.

In that conclusion, you will look upon the One with nail pierced hands. You will see the scars on his brow from the crown of thorns. The wound in his side from the spear.

You will see with your own eyes this baby born in Bethlehem — who went through childhood, baptism, and temptation. Who loved and taught and did miracles. Who was arrested and tried and nailed to a cross. This One who rose from the dead and ascended on high. He will come again, and you will see him come into his rightful throne. Your heart will overflow with gratitude. Your mind will burst with a sudden realization of who this Person is and of what price he paid to bring you to this moment. Your jaw will drop when at long last you see Jesus Christ himself, your brother, your Savior, your friend, and your God—when you see him open wide his arms, and run to you with a smile and embrace that will take your breath away.

You will be reunited with loved ones in Christ who have gone before you. You will recognize them, and they will recognize you. You will still be you, but with all the limiting factors of sin and death finally stripped away, and with all the indescribable blessings of grace added.

And so, you will ever be with the Lord.

Thanks be to God for his unspeakable gift.

I'm satisfied with just a cottage below
A little silver and a little gold.
But in that city where the ransomed will shine
I want a gold one thats silver lined.

I've got a mansion just over the hilltop
In that bright land where we'll never grow old
And someday yonder, we will never more wander
But walk on streets that are pure as gold.

Though often tempted, tormented, and tested
And like the prophet, my pillow's a stone
And though I find here no permanent dwelling
I know He'll give me a mansion my own.

Don't think me poor or deserted or lonely
I'm not discouraged I'm heaven bound
I'm but a pilgrim in search of the city.
I want a mansion, a harp, and a crown.

— IRA F. STANPHILL, 1949

---

1. David H. Wenkel in "The Gnashing of Teeth of Jesus' Opponents," in *Bibliotheca Sacra,* 175 (2018): 83-95.

WHAT'S NEXT

Congratulations! With this book, you have completed the third milestone of the Grace Pathway, "God Grows You." In this milestone, we are filling our hearts and minds with the raw material the Holy Spirit uses to create spiritual growth.

Even though you've completed a milestone, the beautiful thing is we never stop growing with God. We will never fathom the depths of his heart. There is always more to discover, more grace to experience, more truths to believe, more wonders to explore.

We have a whole lifetime to discover the glories of God's heart and the riches of his grace in Christ Jesus.

God is eager for you to know him more and more. I'm praying for you! Keep Growing along the Grace Pathway.

You have now completed lessons in three major milestones:

1. God Saves You (1 red book)
2. God Blesses You (3 blue books)
3. God Grows You (3 green books)

There is one more milestone to go.

Milestone 4 is called "God Uses You."

The grace of God in your life now flows out of and through your life as you serve God from a place of blessing, gratitude and joy.

Here are the books in Milestone 4, God Uses You:

4.1 — Living and Sharing Your Faith

4.2 — Understanding Your Gifts

4.3 — Know Why You Believe (Apologetics)

You've come so far. Keep going and keep growing so you can know all the treasures that are yours because you belong to God.

You'll find these books and more resources at: www.maxgrace.com

If you really want to grow deep in God's Word as preparation for leadership and service in the church, visit the Veritas School of Biblical Ministry, a grace-centered, theological, online school for busy people like you. We believe in Seminary for All. Visit VeritasSchool.life to find out more.